GETTING BY IN
JAPANESE

Second Edition

不二の松

A QUICK BEGINNER'S COURSE FOR
TOURISTS AND BUSINESS PEOPLE

by Charles Inouye
Tufts University

BARRON'S

A Word To The Reader:
Because exchange rates of foreign currencies against the U.S. dollar vary from day to day, the actual cost of a hotel room, taxi ride, or a meal may be more or less than the amounts in the book. Please consult a newspaper, bank, or currency house for the most up-to-date exchange rate.

Acknowledgments
Parts of this book are taken from the first edition by Makiko Haruna. My thanks to Yoshie Kawamura who read the manuscript.

All inquiries should be addressed to:
Barron's Educational Series, Inc.
250 Wireless Boulevard
Hauppauge, New York 11788

Library of Congress Catalog Card No. 96-30042

Library of Congress Cataloging-in-Publication Data
Inouye, Charles Shirō.
    Getting by in Japanese : a quick beginner's course for tourists and business people / Charles Inouye. — 2nd ed.
        p. cm. — (Getting by in —)
    Includes bibliographical references.
    ISBN 0-8120-9687-8 (book). — ISBN 0-8120-8449-7 (book/cassettes package)
    1. Japanese language — Conversation and phrase books — English.
I. Title. II. Series.
PL539.I66   1997
495.6´83421 — dc21   96-30042
                                                       CIP

International Standard Book No. 0-8120-9687-8 (book)
                                 0-8120-8449-7 (book and 2 cassettes)

PRINTED IN HONG KONG
98765432

CONTENTS

THE COURSE. . .
AND HOW TO USE IT

Getting by in Japanese is a six-unit course for anyone planning a visit to Japan. It provides a basic survival kit for some of the crucial situations that typically arise on a visit abroad.

The course

- concentrates on the language you'll need for "getting by" in common situations—negotiating customs, catching a train, meeting people, traveling in Japan, ordering at a restaurant, doing business, shopping, and so on.
- includes real-life conversations recorded by native Japanese speakers.
- encourages you to develop good pronunciation through repeating new words and phrases.

The book includes

- a short outline of Japanese, and the key words and phrases of each unit.
- the texts of the recorded conversations in the order they are presented.
- simple grammatical explanations for deeper understanding of Japanese language structure.
- self-checking exercises for you to do between units, and a short test on the overall course.
- a reference section containing phrases for emergency situations, numbers, days of the week and of the month, months of the year, and a word list of the vocabulary introduced in the chapters.

The two cassettes

- contain six units in dialogue form, designed to allow you to study at your own pace.

To make the most of the course

- Get accustomed to the sounds of the language by listening to the cassettes without referring to the book.
- Take every opportunity to repeat aloud what you are asked to say, and concentrate on listening for key words.
- After each unit, work through the explanations and exercises, and if possible practice the conversations with a friend.
- When you go to Japan, take this book with you, along with a good pocket dictionary and a notebook to jot down the things you discover for yourself.

OUTLINE OF THE JAPANESE LANGUAGE

Japanese differs from English in several ways. The following are some of the characteristics of Japanese.

PRONUNCIATION

SYLLABLES

Japanese syllables end in vowels or a nasal *n*. There are no three-consonant clusters—such as *str* of street in English—and there are no diphthongs (or gliding from one vowel sound to another). Therefore, on first encountering the English word street, a Japanese person would pronounce it as *sutorīto*.

VOWELS

There are five vowels.

a	as in father	**akai** (red)
i	as in each	**ikura** (how much)
u	as in blue	**uta** (song)
e	as in pet	**eki** (station)
o	as in so	**osoi** (slow, late)

Length or duration of vowels plays an important role in Japanese, since two words may differ only in the length of vowels, such as *kūki* (air) and *kuki* (stem). Long vowels are roughly twice as long as short vowels and are represented in this book by a line over the vowel: ā, ī, ū, ē, ō.

Vowels *i* and *u*, when unaccented, tend to be silent after a voiceless sound or between voiceless sounds, for example *sh(i)ta* (below), which sounds like *shta*.

SEMIVOWELS

There are two semivowels: *y* and *w*. They cannot stand as syllables by themselves. Combinations made up of a consonant, a semivowel, and a vowel occur, as in syllables like **kya**. Or, a semivowel and a vowel may make up a syllable like **wa**, which sounds like *wa* in water.

CONSONANTS

There are 14 consonants, most of them found in English. The only two you really have to be careful with are **f** and **r**. Each has a distinctive sound in Japanese, even though both might seem familiar when transliterated into the English alphabet.

f This sound differs from the English *f* sound. When you pronounce it, your lips come close to each other, but your upper teeth do not touch your lower lip. This sound is always followed by *u*, as in *Fujisan* (Mt. Fuji).

r This is neither the English *r* nor *l*, but is a sound between these two. The tip of your tongue moves forward and lightly brushes your alveolar ridge (just behind your upper front teeth).

Double consonants like *tt* in *kitte* (postage stamp) are pronounced with a one-syllable pause between the preceding and following syllable. In other words, *kitte* is three, not two, counts long.

N is often prounced like *m* when it is followed by a *p, b,* or *m* sound, as in *shinbun* (pronounced *shimbun*).

ACCENT

Unlike English, which is stress accented, Japanese is pitch accented. Accented syllables are given a higher pitch, rather than increased volume. Japanese dialects often vary in accent patterns.

THE WRITING SYSTEM

Four different types of script are used in writing Japanese: *hiragana, katakana, kanji* (Chinese characters), and *rōmaji*. Each symbol of *hiragana* and *katakana* stands for a sound, or more precisely one syllable. *Kanji* characters (not included in this book) are assigned phonetic readings, but also possess a meaning. *Rōmaji* utilizes the alphabet to transcribe the Japanese sounds.

Japanese may be written vertically or horizontally. When written vertically from top to bottom, lines proceed from right to left. When written horizontally, lines proceed from left to right, as in English.

For a table of the *hiragana* and *katakana,* please refer to pages 93–96 in the reference section.

STRUCTURE

SYNTAX

Word order is relatively free in Japanese, though a predicate verb or adjective normally ends the sentence. Either of these sentences is grammatical.

Kore wa/akai/n'desu.	This one/red/is.
Akai no wa/kore/desu.	The red one/this/is.

A particle (usually one or two syllables long) that follows a noun specifies some relation between the noun and a predicate verb or adjective. For instance, *wa* marks the topic of a sentence, *ga* the grammatical subject, *o* the object, *ni* the dative, *no* the genitive. Some particles may be dropped in spoken Japanese as long as the intended meaning is understood.

*Kyō **wa**, ikaga desu ka?*	As for today, how is it? (topic)
*Kyō wa, ame **ga** futte imasu.*	Today, it's raining. (subject)

Jā, kono kasa o motte ikimashō.	Well then, let's take this umbrella. (object)
Tanaka-san ni agemashō.	Let's give it to Mr. Tanaka. (dative)
Tanaka-san no kasa desu.	It's Mr. Tanaka's umbrella. (genitive)

Word order does not change in interrogative sentences. When forming a question, put *ka* at the end of the sentence and, if necessary, use a question word like *nani* (what), *itsu* (when), or *doko* (where).

Kore wa pen desu.	This is a pen.
Kore wa pen desu ka?	Is this a pen?

Elements understood by the listener can be omitted in Japanese. You may even omit subjects or objects when you are sure the listener can understand what you are saying.

(Ame ga) futte kimashita.	(The rain) has started falling.
(Kuruma o) kaimashita.	I bought (a car).

GENDER AND ARTICLES

Japanese has neither gender (masculine, feminine, neuter) nor articles (a, an, the).

LEVELS OF FORMALITY

There are numerous levels of formal and informal speech. The main distinction between various levels of formality is the choice of verbs and their conjugations. The conversations in this book are written in the polite or *-masu* form. Most people who speak to you—shopkeepers, clerks, receptionists, waitpersons, business associates—will use polite speech. They will expect this same polite level of speech from you. Generally speaking, women's speech tends to be more polite than men's speech, although this is less true today than it was a decade ago.

Some nouns may be prefixed in polite speech by *o* or *go,* for example, *kanjō/okanjō* (bill) and *hon/gohon* (book). These optional prefixes will be set off by parentheses in this book, as in *(go)hon.*

HONORIFIC VERSUS HUMBLE FORMS

There are two ways to express respect toward a listener or other person. Since respect is expressed by the relative positions of the persons in question, the speaker either "elevates" the other person or "lowers" himself or herself.

• The speaker uses honorific forms to "elevate" someone else. You can use the prefix *o* or *go* when referring to objects associated with the other person. Another way is to choose different verb forms. Rather than say, *kimasu* (come), you would say *irasshaimasu* (come, in the honorific form).

The most important thing to remember is that you never use an honorific form to refer to yourself, members of your family or group, or a thing associated with you or your group. You call someone else *Tanaka-**san*** (**Mr.** Tanaka), but you would never call yourself *Smith-san*. It's Smith, plain and simple.

• The second way is for the speaker to use humble forms to "lower" himself or herself. Someone else might *kimasu* (come) or even *irasshaimasu* (come, in the honorific form). But when referring to oneself, it's *mairimasu* (come, in the humble form) for the very polite.

Because we are concerned here with survival Japanese, we will stick with the polite *-masu* forms. This is perfectly acceptable for non-Japanese who are learning the language.

1 ON ARRIVAL

KEY WORDS AND PHRASES

kore	this one
sore	that one [nearby]
desu	is (polite form of *da*)
Kore wa nan desu ka?	What is this?
ii hoteru	a good hotel
kudasai	please
Ikura desu ka?	How much is it?
shimasu	to do (polite form of *suru*)
hai	all right, I see
iie	no

CONVERSATIONS

GOING THROUGH CUSTOMS

CUSTOMS OFFICER	**Pasupōto wa?** (Your passport?)
TRAVELER	**Kore desu.** (This is it.)
CUSTOMS OFFICER	**(O)nimotsu wa?** (Your luggage?)
TRAVELER	**Kore to sore desu.** (This one and that one.)

CUSTOMS OFFICER **Kore wa nan desu ka?** (What is this?)

TRAVELER **Uisukī desu.** (Whiskey.)

Word List

pasupōto	passport
wa	as for (particle: indicates a topic)
(o)nimotsu	luggage (with polite prefix *o*)
to	and (particle: used to list things)
nan	what
ka	(particle: indicates a question)
uisukī	whiskey

INQUIRING ABOUT HOTELS AT THE AIRPORT

TRAVELER **Ii hoteru o shōkai shite kudasai.** (Please introduce me to a good hotel.)

GUIDE **(O)hitori desu ka.** (One person?)

TRAVELER **Iie, futari desu.** (No. Two people.)

GUIDE **Dono gurai, taizai nasaimasu ka?** (How long will you be staying?)

TRAVELER **Ippaku desu.** (One night.)

GUIDE **Hai, kashikomarimashita.** (I understand.)

Word List

o	(particle: indicates verb object)
shōkai shite	to introduce (the *-te* form of *shōkai suru*)
(o)hitori	one person (with polite prefix *o*)
futari	two persons
dono gurai	how long, how much
taizai nasaimasu	to stay (polite form of *nasaru,* which is an honorific for *suru*)
ippaku	one night
kashikomarimashita	to understand (polite, completed form of *kashikomaru*)

RESERVING AN APPROPRIATE ROOM

GUIDE **Kono hoteru wa, ikaga deshō ka?** (How would you like this hotel?)

TRAVELER **Heya-dai wa ikura desu ka?** (How much is a room?)

GUIDE **Zeikin to sābisu ryō o irete, ippaku ichiman-go-sen en desu.** (With tax and the service charge included, one night is fifteen thousand yen.)

TRAVELER **Sō desu ka? Motto yasui no wa arimasen ka?** (I see. Are there more inexpensive ones?)

GUIDE **Hai. Kono hoteru wa, ippaku has-sen en desu.** (Yes. This other hotel is eight thousand yen a night.)

TRAVELER **Jā, sore ni shimasu.** (Then I'll take that.)

GUIDE **Kashikomarimashita.** (I understand.)

Word List

kono	this
hoteru	hotel
ikaga	how
deshō	is (a polite, speculative form of *desu*)
heya-dai	cost of a room
zeikin	tax
sābisu ryō	service charge
irete	to include (*-te* form of *ireru*)
ichi-man-go-sen en	15,000 yen (see page 96 for numbers)
Sō desu ka?	Is that right?
motto yasui	more inexpensive
no	one (pronoun)
arimasen ka	isn't there?
has-sen en	8,000 yen (see page 96 for numbers)
jā	well then (contraction for *de wa*)
Sore ni shimasu.	I'll take that.

AT THE CURRENCY EXCHANGE WINDOW

CLERK **Irasshaimase.** (Welcome.)

CUSTOMER **Kore o en ni kaete kudasai.** (Please change this to yen.)

CLERK **Hai, kashikomarimashita.** (I understand.)

Word List

irasshaimase	come in, welcome (honorific, imperative for *kuru*)
en	yen
ni	into (particle: indicates the currency into which your dollars are to be changed)
kaete	to change (*-te* form of *kaeru*)

EXPLANATIONS

DESU

The verb *desu* is used frequently. In its various conjugations, it indicates being: am, is, are, was, were, been, be.

When you pronounce *desu,* the final *u* is usually silent.

> *Sumisu desu.* [I] am Smith.
> *Nihonjin desu.* [I] am Japanese.
> *Amerikajin desu.* [I] am American.

Desu becomes *deshita* in its completed form, and *deshō* in its tentative or speculative form. The informal or dictionary form of *desu* is *da*.

SHIMASU: POLITENESS AND VERBS

You choose different verbs according to who is doing the action. Consider these three different words for the verb "to do."

honorific	nasaimasu	**Shachō ga nasaimasu.**
(what somebody else does)		The President will do it.
neutral	shimasu	**Tanaka-san ga shimasu.**
		Mr. Tanaka will do it.
humble	itashimasu	**Watakushi ga itashimasu.**
(what you do)		I'll do it.

You can be polite by either raising someone else's position by using honorific verbs, or by lowering your own by using humble verbs.

Notice that verbs in all three examples are in the polite *desu/masu* form. The dictionary (infinitive) form of these same three verbs would be *nasaru, suru,* and *itasu.*

THE -*MASU* CONJUGATION OF VERBS

The polite -*masu* conjugation of verbs is the one you'll be using most. It is formed for the three types of Japanese verbs as follows:

Vowel Verbs

These end in *e* + *ru* or *i* + *ru,* such as *taberu* (to eat) and *miru* (to see). For the -*masu* conjugation, simply drop the *ru* and add *masu.*

Dictionary Form	**-*masu* Form**	
tabe-ru	*tabe-masu*	to eat
mi-ru	*mi-masu*	to see

Consonant Verbs

These end in -*ku, -gu, -bu, -mu, -nu;* a vowel + *ru;* a vowel + *u; -su, -tsu.* To form the -*masu* conjugation, change the final syllable in this manner:

start with the verb	*iku*		
drop the *u*	*ik*		
add *i*	*iki*		
add *masu*.	*ikimasu*		

Note that for *-su* and *-tsu*, *-su* changes to *shi* (rather than *si*), and *-tsu* changes to *-chi*.

Verb Ending	Verb	-masu Form	
-ku	*kaku*	*kakimasu*	to write
-gu	*isogu*	*isogimasu*	to hurry
-bu	*yobu*	*yobimasu*	to call
-mu	*nomu*	*nomimasu*	to drink
-nu	*shinu*	*shinimasu*	to die
vowel + *ru*	*kaeru*	*kaerimasu*	to return
vowel + *u*	*kau*	*ka(w)imasu**	to buy
-su	*hanasu*	*hanashimasu*	to speak
-tsu	*matsu*	*machimasu*	to wait

Irregular Verbs

Memorize the *-masu* forms of *suru* and *kuru*.

suru	*shimasu*	to do
kuru	*kimasu*	to come

THE *-TE* FORM OF VERBS

The *-te* form of verbs is frequently used in combination with other verbs. Standing alone, it can indicate a simple imperative, e.g., *suru*—to do—becomes *shite*—do it. Most often, though, it is followed by another verb or phrase.

To make the *-te* form:

*Note: The *w* disappears in *kaimasu*.

Vowel Verbs

Change the final *ru* into *te*.

-eru	*taberu*	*tabete*	to eat
-iru	*miru*	*mite*	to see

Consonant Verbs

Change the final syllables according to the patterns below:

-ku	*kaku*	*kaite*	to write
-gu	*isogu*	*isoide*	to hurry
-bu	*yobu*	*yonde*	to call
-mu	*nomu*	*nonde*	to drink
-nu	*shinu*	*shinde*	to die
–vowel + ru	*kaeru*	*kaette*	to return
–vowel + u	*kau*	*katte*	to buy
-tsu	*matsu*	*matte*	to wait

Irregular Verbs

Memorize the *-te* forms.

suru	*shite*	to do
kuru	*kite*	to come

Polite Requests

With the *-te* form, you can make polite requests. Simply add auxiliary verbs such as *kudasai* (please) or *itadakemasen ka* (Could I have you . . .).

VERB in the *-te* form + *kudasai* = "Please VERB."

taberu/tabemasu	*tabete*	*Tabete kudasai.*	Please eat [it].
kiru/kimasu	*kite*	*Kite kudasai.*	Please wear [this].
kaku/kakimasu	*kaite*	*Kaite kudasai.*	Please write [something].
isogu/isogimasu	*isoide*	*Isoide kudasai.*	Please hurry.
yobu/yobimasu	*yonde*	*Yonde kudasai.*	Please call her.

nomu/nomimasu	*nonde*	*Nonde kudasai.*	Please drink [it].
shinu/shinimasu	*shinde*	*Shinde kudasai.*	Please die.
kaeru/kaerimasu	*kaette*	*Kaette kudasai.*	Please return.
kau/kaimasu	*katte*	*Katte kudasai.*	Please buy [it].
matsu/machimasu	*matte*	*Matte kudasai.*	Please wait.
suru/shimasu	*shite*	*Shite kudasai.*	Please do [it].
kuru/kimasu	*kite*	*Kite kudasai.*	Please come.

VERB *-te* form + *itadaku/itadakimasu* = "I'd like you to VERB"

VERB *-te* form + *itadakemasen ka?* = "Could I have you VERB for me?"

Note: When making requests, it is customary to use a negative, potential form of *itadakimasu*—thus, *itadakemasen ka?*

Tabete itadakimasu.	I'd like you to eat [it].
Tabete itadakemasen ka?	Could I have you eat [it] for me?
Kite itadakimasu.	I'd like you to wear [this].
Kite itadakemasen ka?	Could I have you wear [this] for me?

And so on.

DEMONSTRATIVE PRONOUNS AND ADJECTIVES

Demonstrative pronouns change according to the distance from the speaker to the thing being pointed out.

kore	this	*Kore wa nan desu ka?*	What is this?
sore	that	*Sore wa nan desu ka?*	What is that?
are	that over there	*Are wa nan desu ka?*	What is that over there?
dore	which	*Dore desu ka?*	Which is it?

Demonstrative pronouns can stand alone. Other demonstratives are adjectival and precede nouns.

kono *hoteru*	this hotel
Kono hoteru wa yasui desu.	This hotel is inexpensive.
sono *hoteru*	that hotel
Sono hoteru wa ii desu ka?	Is that hotel acceptable?
ano *hoteru*	that hotel
Ano hoteru wa takai desu.	That hotel (we talked about) is expensive.
dono *hoteru*	which hotel?
Dono hoteru ga ii n' desu ka?	Which hotel is good?

Note the phonetic pattern of the consonants *k, s, a, d*. The same is retained in demonstrative pronouns for place.

koko	here	*Koko desu.*	It's here.
soko	there	*Soko desu.*	It's there.
asoko	over there	*Asoko desu.*	It's over there.
doko	where	*Doko desu ka?*	Where is it?

PARTICLES

Particles are short—one- or two-syllable words—that have a variety of meanings and functions. Many act like prepositions—to, at, toward, etc.—but others have a wider grammatical force, indicating a question, a topic, a subject, and so on. Some have more than one meaning, like *kara* and *to*. And some combine with others, for example, *to wa*. Here are some of the most frequently used particles and some of their meanings.

de	at (place of action)
Hoteru de tabemasu.	I'll eat at the hotel.
e	to (movement toward)
Heya e ikimasu.	I will go to my room.
ga	(the subject)
Pasupōto ga arimasen.	I don't have a passport.

ka	(a question)
Nan desu ka?	What is it?
kara	from (a starting point)
Hikōjo kara kimashita.	I came from the airport.
kara	because (a reason)
Futari desu kara . . .	Since there are two of us . . .
made	until (a limit)
Hoteru made ikimasu.	I'm going as far as the hotel.
mo	also (inclusive listing)
Uisukī mo arimasu.	I also have whiskey.
to	and (listing)
Uisukī to nimotsu desu.	It's whiskey and luggage.
to	(cognition, speech)
Ii to omoimasu.	I think it's good.
wa	(topic of sentence)
Nimotsu wa, kore to sore.	As for my luggage, this and that.

THE O AND GO PREFIXES

Some nouns, such as *(o)nimotsu* (luggage), *(o)hitori* (one person) are preceded by the prefix *o.* Adding *o* or *go* increases politeness and is used when referring to someone else, or to things related to someone else. Women still use these prefixes more than men, who tend to be less polite in speech. But their use by both sexes is common and frequent.

Some words, such as *(go)han* (cooked rice) and *(o)cha* (tea), are almost never used without a polite prefix. Others, such as *(o)kōcha* (English tea), are variable. You shouldn't use *o* for everything just because you want to be polite. Better to learn the appropriate cases as situations arise. Above all, try not to exhalt yourself. Someone else's luggage is *(o)nimotsu,* but your own is *nimotsu.*

YES AND NO

Hai means "yes." *Iie* means "no." The less formal forms are *ee* or *un* for "yes," and *iya* for "no." These informal terms should be avoided unless you know the person with whom you are speaking very well.

You will notice that in Japanese conversation, the listener does not simply listen quietly but confirms what is being said by punctuating the discourse with *hai, ee, Sō desu ka?* (Is that right?) or some other short word or phrase. In this context, they mean "all right, I see."

CARDINAL NUMBERS

Japanese uses two methods for counting—the Japanese and the Chinese systems. The Japanese system goes up to ten. Use these numbers when you do not need to use a counter to specify what it is that you're counting. Say, for instance, *Hitotsu kudasai.* (I'd like one, please) rather than *Ichi-mai kudasai.* (I'd like one sheet.) (Here, *mai* is the counter for sheetlike objects.)

hitotsu	1	*muttsu*	6
futatsu	2	*nanatsu*	7
mittsu	3	*yattsu*	8
yottsu	4	*kokonotsu*	9
itsutsu	5	*tō*	10

The Chinese style of counting allows you to say much larger numbers. Add counters to these to be more specific: *San-mai kudasai.* (I'd like three sheets, please.)

ichi	1	*jū-ichi*	11
ni	2	*jū-ni*	12
san	3	*jū-san*	13
shi, yon	4	*jū-shi (jū-yon)*	14
go	5	*jū-go*	15
roku	6	*jū-roku*	16
shichi, nana	7	*jū-shichi (jū-nana)*	17
hachi	8	*jū-hachi*	18
ku, kyū	9	*jū-ku (jū-kyū)*	19
jū	10	*ni-jū*	20

ni-jū-ichi, ni-jū-ni . . .	21, 22, and so on
san-jū	30
yon-jū	40
go-jū	50
roku-jū	60
nana-jū	70
hachi-jū	80
kyū-jū	90
hyaku	100
hyaku-jū, hyaku-ni-jū . . .	110, 120, and so on
ni-hyaku, san-byaku, yon-hyaku . . .	200, 300, 400, and so on
sen	1,000
sen-hyaku, sen-ni-hyaku . . .	1,100, 1,200, and so on
ni-sen, san-zen . . .	2,000, 3,000 and so on
ichi-man	10,000
ichi-man-is-sen, ichi-man-ni-sen	11,000, 12,000, and so on
ni-man, san-man . . .	20,000, 30,000, and so on
hyaku-man	1,000,000

EXERCISES

Answers are on page 26.

1. Form these simple sentences.
   a. I'm Smith. (*Sumisu*)
   b. It's a passport. (*pasupōto*)
   c. It's whiskey. (*uisukī*)
   d. Its luggage. (*nimotsu*)

2. Can you request that someone do the following actions?
   a. to see (*miru*)
   b. to eat (*taberu*)
   c. to hurry (*isogu*)
   d. to buy (*kau*)

3. Now you know how to ask someone what things are. Try these.
   a. What is this?
   b. What is that? (near you)
   c. What is that? (over there)
   d. Which one (do you mean)?

4. You're reserving a room. You ask how much one night's lodging will cost: *Ippaku wa, ikura desu ka?* Convert the following answers into numbers you know. See page 96 (and the top of every page) for number equivalents.
   a. *Go-sen en desu.*
   b. *Ichi-man en desu.*
   c. *Kyū-sen en desu.*
   d. *Has-sen go-hyaku en desu.*

WORTH KNOWING

CUSTOMS

Don't even think about taking illegal drugs—marijuana, cocaine, etc.—to Japan. Penalties are severe.

MAJOR INTERNATIONAL AIRPORTS

There are two major airports in Japan: the Narita International Airport near Tokyo, and the Kansai International Airport near Osaka. English is spoken at both, so you should have few problems going through customs and passport control. The Japan Travel Bureau (*Kōtsūkōsha*) has offices, open 24 hours, at these airports. They are staffed with English speakers who will be happy to help you with ground transportation or with hotel reservations if you haven't made them in advance.

To get to Tokyo from Narita, there is a Keisei express train to Ueno, and a JR express to Tokyo and Shinjuku. You can also take the "limousine," a special airport bus, to the Tokyo City Air Terminal or to six other destinations in the city. Once you get to the city, take a taxi to your hotel. (See map on page 121.) From the Kansai Airport to Osaka, Kobe, and Kyoto, take the Haruka express train, which leaves from the terminal. (See map on page 122).

Making connecting flights to other cities in Japan is difficult since most domestic flights leave from either the Haneda Airport, in Tokyo, or the Itami Airport, north of Osaka.

If you have a lot of luggage, try having it forwarded by express mail from the airport. This service is fast and reliable. On your return flight, have your luggage forwarded so that you can pick it up at the airport when you get there.

BEING POLITE

As in English, polite language distances you from others, while informal language indicates either intimacy or a clearly differentiated level of power. Strangers speak formally to each other, while friends speak informally with each other. Or when the relationship is unequal, that is, one side is clearly more powerful than the other, a mix of politeness levels can be heard—a superior speaking informally to a subordinate, who speaks back politely.

Ultimately, it is good to master all levels of politeness. But for getting by, stick with *desu/masu*. That's what the Japanese will expect of someone new to their culture.

CATEGORIES OF ACCOMMODATIONS

The present yen-dollar exchange makes staying in Japan suprisingly expensive. Fortunately, as in the United States, there are a wide variety of hotels to choose from. Due to a lack of space, luxury hotels are comparable in service but more costly and less spacious than their American analogues. Room service for both Western and Japanese cuisine is available, as well as numerous dining and shopping options, laundry and dry cleaning, taxi and limousine service, and tours. Bilingual (Japanese and English) telephone, television, video, and information brochures are provided. Options for exercise are limited.

If you don't mind being cramped, there are several types of economy hotels, especially in the larger cities. Some are called business hotels (*bijinesu hoteru*). They cater to business people who need no more than a bed, a private bathroom, a telephone, and a television. Some chains have inexpensive weekly and monthly rates. There are even more cramped capsule hotels (*kyapuseru hoteru*), which offer not much more than a small closet to hang your suit and a bunk bed to crawl into. And finally, there are the so-called love hotels (*rabu hoteru*), which charge by the hour.

Hotels are relatively new to Japan and are modeled after Western models. Inns, on the other hand, have been around for a long time and still reflect a more traditional lifestyle. You might prefer sleeping in a *futon* laid out on a tatami-mat floor, taking hot baths in a communal tub, and eating Japanese breakfasts and dinners (which can be sumptuous if you're up to the adventure). You'll find inns in the country, often clustered around hot springs, although cities like Kyoto have their share. They're definitely worth a try if you have the time and are willing to experience something different.

Inexpensive youth hostels are also available, as are tax-subsidized lodgings for Japanese citizens (who can entertain foreign guests).

ADDITIONAL VOCABULARY

beddo	bed
chūshoku, asa (go)han	breakfast
chūshoku, hiru (go)han	lunch
danbō	heating
denwa	telephone

dorai-kurīningu	dry cleaning
eiga	movie
erebētā	elevator
futon	Japanese-style bed
hijōguchi	emergency exit
kagi	key
kaidan	stairs
kyanseru, torikeshi	cancel
makura	pillow
mōfu	blanket
(o)tearai, toire	toilet
rūmu sābisu	room service
ryokan	Japanese-style inn
sentaku	laundry
terebi	television
uketsuke	reception
washitsu	Japanese-style room
yōshitsu	Western-style room
yūshoku, yūgohan	dinner

ANSWERS TO EXERCISES

1. a. *Sumisu desu.* b. *Pasupōto desu.*
   c. *Uisukī desu.* d. *Nimotsu desu.*
2. a. *Mite kudasai.* b. *Tabete kudasai.*
   c. *Isoide kudasai.* d. *Katte kudasai.*
3. a. *Kore wa nan desu ka?*
   b. *Sore wa nan desu ka?*
   c. *Are wa nan desu ka?*
   d. *Dore desu ka?*
4. a. 5,000 yen. b. 10,000 yen.
   c. 9,000 yen. d. 8,500 yen.

2 MEETING PEOPLE

KEY WORDS AND PHRASES

Hajimemashite.	How do you do?
Yoroshiku onegai shimasu.	Pleased to make your acquaintance.
Konban wa.	Good evening.
Arigatō gozaimasu.	Thank you. (humble, polite form of *arigatai n'desu*)
Ojama itashimasu.	Forgive the intrusion. (humble, polite form of *jama suru*)
Sumimasen.	Excuse me. Sorry.
Ii desu nē.	It's great.
Nihon	Japan
Nihongo	Japanese language
jōzu	good at, skillful
Shitsurei shimasu.	It's time for me to leave.
Ashita wa hayai desu kara.	I have to get up early tomorrow morning [so I'd better be going].

CONVERSATIONS

GLAD TO MEET YOU

VISITOR **Hajimemashite. Watakushi, Tomasu Shapairo to mōshimasu.** (How do you do. I'm Tom Shapiro.)

HOST **Hajimemashite. Shimizu Junko desu.** (Glad to meet you. I'm Junko Shimizu.)

VISITOR **Dōzo yoroshiku onegai shimasu.** (Pleased to make your acquaintance.)

HOST **Kochira koso. Dōzo yoroshiku.** (The pleasure is mine.)

Word List

watakushi	I (polite)
to	(particle: indicates what is said)
mōshimasu	to call (polite form of *mōsu*, which is the humble verb for *iu*)
Shimizu Junko	Junko Shimizu (surname comes first in Japanese usage)
dōzo	please
Kochira koso.	Same here.

EXCHANGING GREETINGS

TANAKA **Ohayō gozaimasu.** (Good morning.)

SMITH **Ohayō gozaimasu.** (Good morning.)

TANAKA **(O)genki desu ka?** (How are you?)

SMITH **Genki desu. Okagesama de. . .** (I am fine. Thanks to you.)

Word List

Ohayō gozaimasu.	Good morning. (polite, humble form of *hayai*)
(O)genki	Good spirits.
Okagesama de	Thanks to you.

ENTERING SOMEONE'S HOUSE

GUEST **Konban wa.** (Good evening.)

HOST **Yoku irasshaimashita. Dōzo oagari kudasai.**
(Thanks for coming. Please, come in.)

GUEST **Ojama shimasu.** (Forgive the intrusion.)

HOST **Sumimasen ga, surippa o dōzo** (Sorry, but here
are some slippers [if you could indulge us]).

GUEST **Arigatō gozaimasu.** [Handing a gift to your host
or hostess.] **Kore, nani mo nai n'desu ga,
dōzo** ... (Thank you. This is nothing much, but
please ....)

Word List

Konban wa.	Good evening.
Yoku irasshaimashita.	Thanks for coming.
dōzo	please [come in]
oagari kudasai	come in (honorific, imperative form of *agaru*)
ga	but
surippa	slippers
nani mo nai	nothing much
dōzo	please [accept it]
n'desu	contraction for *no desu*

WHAT DO YOU THINK ABOUT JAPAN?

HOST **Nihon wa, dō desu ka?** (What do you think
about Japan?)

GUEST **Ii desu nē.** (It's great.)

HOST **Sō desu ka? Demo, kochira wa semai deshō.**
(Really, but don't you find it crowded?)

GUEST **Iie. Sō de mo arimasen. Tabemono mo oishii
desu.** (No. Not really. And the food is delicious.)

Word List

dō	how (less formal than *ikaga*)
Sō desu ka?	Is that right?
demo	but
kochira	here (a polite form of *koko*)
semai	crowded
deshō	isn't it (a speculative form of *desu*)
Sō de mo arimasen.	Not necessarily.
tabemono	food
mo	also
oishii	delicious

YOUR JAPANESE IS EXCELLENT

HOST   **Nihongo ga (o)jōzu desu nē!** (Your Japanese is good. It really is!)

GUEST   **Iie, amari jōzu de wa arimasen.** (No, it's not so good.)

HOST   **Yappari, muzukashii desu ka?** (So it really is difficult?)

GUEST   **Muzukashii desu nē**. (It really is difficult.)

Word List

nē	aren't you, right (particle: seeks confirmation, agreement)
amari	[not] very (when used with *de wa arimasen* or other negative verbs and adjectives)
yappari	as expected
muzukashii	difficult

SAYING GOODBYE

GUEST   **Mō, sorosoro shitsurei shimasu.** (We should start thinking about getting back.)

HOST   **Sō desu ka?** (Really?)

GUEST **Ashita wa hayai desu kara.** (I have an early start tomorrow.)

HOST **Jā, mata. Chikai uchi ni.** (Well then, see you again. Soon.)

GUEST **Kyō wa, hontō ni arigatō gozaimashita.** (Thanks for everything today.)

Word List

mō	already
sorosoro	it's about time, by and by
shitsurei shimasu	to take one's leave (polite form of *shitsurei suru*)
ashita	tomorrow
hayai	early
desu kara	because
jā, mata	well, [we'll have to do this] again
chikai uchi ni	before too long
kyō wa	as for today
hontō ni	truly

EXPLANATIONS

NAMES

Japanese give their surnames first, followed by a given name or title. For example, in "*Shimizu Junko desu*," Junko is the given name and Shimizu is the family name. When titles are used, they follow the surname, as in *Tsuruga-shachō*, or President Tsuruga.

When introducing yourself, it is usually enough to give your surname, "Shapiro *desu*." But in those cases when you give your full name, you should retain the natural order, "Tom Shapiro" rather than "Shapiro Tom."

PRONOUNS

Pronouns are used much less frequently in Japanese than in English. Pronouns for "you" and "I" are often avoided, though not in the first dialogue where the speaker is identifying himself. The general lack of pronouns in everyday speech causes less confusion than you might expect since the politeness level of verbs indicates who is speaking or being spoken about.

INTRODUCTIONS

When giving your name, you can use a humble verb, "*Sumisu to mōshimasu*," or just plain "*Sumisu desu*." Either is fine.

Say *hajimemashite* if meeting someone for the first time. Finish off an introduction with *Dōzo yoroshiku onegai shimasu*. (Pleased to make your acquaintance.) The implication here is that your relationship, now newly established, will continue in the future, and that you'll need the other person's good will (and maybe even their cooperation or help). You can shorten this to *dōzo yoroshiku* or *yoroshiku onegai shimasu*.

SUMIMASEN

Sumimasen is a word you'll use frequently. To get another's attention, you can say *Sumimasen*. If you bump into someone, you say *Sumimasen* or *Sumimasen deshita* (in the completed form). When someone does something for you, say *Sumimasen*. The usage of this important word is much like that of the English word "sorry"—sorry to bother you; sorry about that; sorry to put you out; and so on.

SAYING THANKS

As in English, there are many ways to say thanks. Here are some, from the most abbreviated to the more extended and, therefore, formal ways.

Dōmo.	Thanks alot.
Arigatō.	Thanks.
Arigatō gozaimasu.	Thank you.
Dōmo arigatō gozaimasu.	Thank you very much.
Dōmo, hontō ni arigatō gozaimasu.	[I'm] truly grateful for your kindness.

EMPHASIS

In colloquial Japanese, sentences often end with various combinations of particles, such as *nē* and *yo*. These control the forcefulness and the mode of a sentence—whether you're posing a question, making an accusation, giving an order, and so forth. As you might imagine, intonation plays a major role in determining their meaning as well, making the various nuances innumerable.

Without getting into all the subtleties, you should know that the exclamatory word *nē* is frequently used, particularly when the sentence or phrase uses an adjective, as in "*Ii desu nē.*" It solicits the listener's agreement. But is used more frequently than the English, "isn't it?"

Yo is more forceful, more like an exclamation point. Depending on the intonation of the sentence, *yo* can express either enthusiasm (rising) or perturbation (falling).

Rising tone:	*Mō shimashita yo!*	I did it already [so everything's set]!
Falling tone:	*Mō shimashita yo!*	I did it already [so get off my back]!

The use of this particle becomes habitual for many non-native speakers, straining to be understood. But you should avoid its overuse.

OTHER FORMS OF DEMONSTRATIVE PRONOUNS

There are informal and formal forms for the demonstrative pronouns of place you have learned.

	Regular	**Informal**	**Formal**
here	*koko*	*kotchi*	*kochira*
there	*soko*	*sotchi*	*sochira*
over there	*asoko*	*atchi*	*achira*
which	*dono*	*dotchi*	*dochira*

EXERCISES

Answers are on page 38.

1. Introduce yourself as if you were the following people:
   a. Michael Johnson
   b. Sandra Buckley
   c. Bill Clinton
   d. Gordon Hinkley

2. Someone says good morning to you. How do you respond?
   FRIEND   *Ohayō gozaimasu.*
   a. (Good morning.)
   FRIEND   *Ogenki desu ka?*
   b. (I feel great. Thanks to you.)

3. You are entering someone's house. Respond to the following cues.
   HOST   *Konban wa.*
   a. (Good evening.)
   HOST   *Yoku irasshaimashita. Dōzo oagari kudasai.*
   b. (Forgive the intrusion.)
   HOST   *Sumimasen ga, surippa o dōzo.*
   c. (Thank you very much.)

4. Your host asks you about your impressions of Japan. Tell him or her that you think Japan is a _____ place (*tokoro*).

HOST *Nihon wa, ikaga desu ka?*
a. a good (place) (*ii*)
b. hot/cold (*atsui/samui*)
c. attractive, clean (*kirei*)
d. interesting (*omoshiroi*)

5. Someone compliments your almost non-existent Japanese. You humbly reply.
   HOST *Nihongo ga (o)jōzu desu nē.*
   a. (No, I'm not very good at it.)
   HOST *Yappari, muzukashii desu ka?*
   b. (Yes, it is difficult.)

6. You're at a gathering. Tell your host you have to be going since you have to get started early the next morning.
   a. (I should be leaving.)
   HOST *Sō desu ka?*
   b. (I've got to get up early tomorrow.)
   HOST *Jā mata. Chikai uchi ni.*
   c. (Thanks for a great day.)

WORTH KNOWING

ENTERTAINING GUESTS

Entertaining at one's home occurs less frequently in Japan than in the United States, so when it does happen it should be considered a special privilege. It is more common to entertain at a restaurant, at a coffee shop, or at a private bar.

YOUR JAPANESE IS SO GOOD!

For various reasons, some Japanese do not expect foreigners to speak to them in their language, even though the number of non-Japanese who do is increasing steadily.

Don't be surprised when you are praised for saying (or reading) even the most rudimentary things. The gracious way to deal with undeserved praise is to state the truth: "*Iie, jōzu de wa arimasen.* (No, I'm not very good)."

TAKING YOUR SHOES OFF

Take your shoes off whenever you enter buildings with a *genkan* (lowered portico). Such places include houses, Japanese-style restaurants and inns, temples, and elementary schools.

Shoes are worn in most public buildings, hotels, Western-style restaurants, and the like. It's a good idea to wear shoes that are easy to put on and take off, and to give some thought to what you are wearing beneath them. It's considered gauche not to wear stockings.

NOTHING MUCH

Take a gift with you when visiting someone's home. Gift giving is an important part of social practice: you'll probably be the recipient of many acts of generosity, so you'll want to have some way of reciprocating. It is important to have things properly wrapped, and to speak humbly of your ability to match someone else's kindness. Thus, your gift to your host is *nani mo arimasen* (nothing much). For a list of appropriate gifts, see page 75.

When giving a gift, it is proper etiquette to use two hands.

ADDITIONAL VOCABULARY

ane	one's own older sister (compare *onēsan*)
ani	one's own older brother (compare *onīsan*)
chichi	one's own father (compare *otōsan*)
genkan	portico
haha	one's own mother (compare *okāsan*)
hōmu pātī	entertaining at one's home
imōto	younger sister
jiko shōkai	self introduction
kazoku	family
kutsu	shoes
kutsu bera	shoehorn
kyōdai	siblings
musuko	son
musume	daughter
nyōbō	one's own wife
obasan	someone's aunt
obāsan	someone's grandmother
ojisan	uncle
ojīsan	someone's grandfather
okāsan	someone's mother (compare *haha*)
onēsan	someone's older sister
onīsan	someone's older brother
otōsan	someone's father
otōto	younger brother
settai suru	to entertain
shōtai suru	to invite
shujin	husband
tatami	rice-straw mat
tomodachi, yūjin	friend
uchi	house
zabuton	a cushion

ANSWERS TO EXERCISES

1. a. *Hajimemashite, Maikeru Jonson desu. Dōzo yoroshiku.*
   b. *Hajimemashite, Sandora Bakuri desu. Dōzo yoroshiku.*
   c. *Hajimemashite, Biru Kurinton desu. Dōzo yoroshiku.*
   d. *Hajimemashite, Gōdan Hinkuri desu. Dōzo yoroshiku.*
2. a. *Ohayō gozaimasu.* b. *Ee Okagesama de.*
3. a. *Konban wa.* b. *Ojama itashimasu.*
   c. *Arigatō gozaimasu.*
4. a. *Ii tokoro desu nē.* b. *Atsui / samui tokoro desu nē.* c. *Kirei na tokoro desu nē.* d. *Omoshiroi tokoro desu nē.*
5. a. *Iie, jōzu de wa arimasen.*
   b. *Muzukashii desu nē.*
6. a. *Sorosoro, shitsurei shimasu.*
   b. *Ashita wa, hayai desu kara.*
   c. *Kyō wa, hontō ni arigatō gozaimashita.*

3 GETTING AROUND

KEY WORDS AND PHRASES

(Noun) wa, doko desu ka?	Where is …?
Dō itashimashite.	You're welcome.
(Noun) made, ikura desu ka?	How much is it to …?
Onegai shimasu.	Please [I'll take that].
(Noun) made, itte kudasai.	Please take me to ….
(Noun) made, dō ikeba ii n'desu ka?	How do I get to …?
(Noun) ni tomarimasu ka?	Does [this bus] stop at …?

CONVERSATIONS

WHERE CAN I BUY A TRAIN OR BUS TICKET?

TRAVELER **Sumimasen. Kippu-uriba wa doko desu ka?** (Excuse me. Where do they sell bus tickets?)

PASSERBY **Asoko desu.** (Over there.)

TRAVELER **Dōmo arigatō.** (Thank you.)

PASSERBY **Dō itashimashite.** (You're welcome.)

Word List

kippu	ticket
uriba	selling place

HOW MUCH IS IT TO SHIBUYA
(ON THE SUBWAY)?

TRAVELER **Sumimasen. Shibuya made, ikura desu ka?**
(Excuse me. How much is it to Shibuya?)

PASSERBY **Shibuya desu ka? Ni-hyaku-en desu.**
(Shibuya? 200 yen.)

TRAVELER **Ni-hyaku-en desu ka? Dōmo arigatō
gozaimashita.** (Two hundred yen? Thank you
very much.)

Word List

Shibuya	Shibuya Station (in Tokyo)
ni-hyaku en	200 yen
made	until, up to, as far as (particle: indicates distance)

COULD I GET EXPRESS TICKETS TO ATAMI?

TRAVELER **Atami made, ōfuku de, otona ichi-mai to,
kodomo ni-mai kudasai. Tokkyū ken mo
onegai shimasu.** (Round trip to Atami. One
adult and two children, please. And could I also
get special express tickets?)

CLERK **Shitei-seki desu ka?** (Reserved seats?)

TRAVELER **Hai. Kin'enseki o onegai shimasu.** (Yes. No
smoking, please.)

CLERK **Sore dewa, jōshaken to tokkyū ken to
shitēseki ken desu.** (So, here are your regular
tickets, and your special express reserved seat
tickets.)

Word List

Atami	(name of a place)
ōfuku	round trip
otona	adult

ichi-mai	one ticket
kodomo	child
ni-mai	two tickets
tokkyū ken	special express tickets (paid for in addition to regular fare)
jōshaken	regular railway ticket (determined by the mileage)
irimasu	to need (polite form of *iru*)
shitei-seki	reserved seat
kin'enseki	non-smoking seat

RIDING IN A TAXI: PLEASE TAKE ME TO THIS ADDRESS

DRIVER **Dochira made desu ka?** (Where are we going?)

PASSENGER **Kono jūsho made, itte kudasai.** (Take me to this address, please.)

Word List

kono jūsho	this address
itte	to go (*-te* form of *iku*)

ON FOOT: HOW DO I GET TO THE GOLDEN PAVILION?

TRAVELER **Kinkaku-ji wa, dō ikeba ii n'desu ka?** (How do I get to the Golden Pavilion?)

PASSERBY **Kono michi o massugu itte, futatsu-me no shingō o migi ni magatta tokoro desu.** (Go straight down this road. At the second light, turn right and you're there.)

TRAVELER **Wakarimashita. Dōmo arigatō gozaimashita.** (Yes, I understand. Thank you very much.)

PASSERBY **Dō itashimashite.** (My pleasure.)

Word List

Kinkaku-ji	The Golden Pavilion (in Kyoto)
dō ikeba	how should I go (conditional form of *iku*)
ii	good
michi	road
massugu	straight ahead
itte	to go (*te* form of *iku*)
futatsu-me	the second
no	(particle: shows possession)
shingō	traffic light
migi	right
ni	(particle: to, toward)
magatta	to turn (completed form of *magaru*)
tokoro	place

DOES THIS BUS GO TO TACHIKAWA?

TRAVELER **Sumimasen. Kono basu wa, Tachikawa ni ikimasu ka?** (Excuse me. Does this bus go to Tachikawa?)

PASSERBY **Hai. Ni-ban basu wa ikimasu.** (Yes. Number 2 bus goes there.)

TRAVELER **Kunitachi ni mo tomarimasu ka?** (Does it also stop in Kunitachi?)

PASSERBY **Hai. Tomaru to omoimasu.** (Yes. I think it stops there.)

TRAVELER **Arigatō gozaimashita.** (Thank you.)

Word List

basu	bus
Tachikawa	Tachikawa (a city west of Tokyo)
ikimasu	to go (polite form of *iku*)
ni-ban	number two
Kunitachi	Kunitachi (a city west of Tokyo)
ni	at (particle: indicates a place)

tomarimasu	to stop (polite form of *tomaru*)
to	(particle: indicates cognition)
omoimasu	to think (polite form of *omou*)
arigatō gozaimashita	thank you (completed form of *arigatō goza-imasu*)

EXPLANATIONS

WHERE IS THE TICKET WINDOW?

Being able to ask where something is will be very useful to you. The pattern is as follows:

NOUN + *wa, doko desu ka?* = "Where is NOUN?"

Kippu uriba wa, doko desu ka?	Where is the ticket window?
Osaka wa, doko desu ka?	Where is Osaka?

As already introduced, *doko* belongs to a group of demonstratives for place. To your question "*Doko desu ka?*" the answer might be one of the following.

Koko desu.	Right here.
Soko desu.	There.
Asoko desu.	Over there.

THE PARTICLE *MADE*

Made indicates an upper limit of some sort. When asking for train fares to various places, you can use the following pattern.

NOUN + *made, ikura desu ka?* = "How much is it, to go as far as NOUN?"

Or when you're riding in a taxi, you can instruct the driver to take you as far as a certain place. Here's the pattern:

NOUN + *made, itte kudasai.* = "Please go as far as NOUN."

-*MAI* AND OTHER COUNTERS

A counter is a word that follows a number to show the type or class of the item being counted. The suffix -*mai* is such a counter. In English, we say two "sheets" of paper, or three "head" of cattle. In Japan, we use -*mai* for thin, flat objects, such as tickets and pieces of paper. For long, cylindrical objects, such as pencils and bottles -*hon* is used. For people, -*nin* is used. Use the Chinese style numbers *ichi, ni, san, shi* (rather than *hitotsu, futatsu, mittsu, yottsu*) with counters. Once again, for a list of numbers, see pages 96–98.

ORDINAL NUMBERS

There are two ways to create ordinal numbers, depending on whether you are using the Japanese or Chinese style of counting.

For Japanese numbers, add the suffix -*me,* as follows:

hitotsu	1	*hitotsu-me*	first
futatsu	2	*futatsu-me*	second
mittsu	3	*mittsu-me*	third
yottsu	4	*yottsu-me*	fourth
itsutsu	5	*itsutsu-me*	fifth
muttsu	6	*muttsu-me*	sixth
nanatsu	7	*nanatsu-me*	seventh
yattsu	8	*yattsu-me*	eighth
kokonotsu	9	*kokonotsu-me*	ninth
tō	10	*jūban-me*	tenth

Note that Japanese ordinal numbers work only up to nine. Thereafter, you will have to change to the Chinese system.

For Chinese-style numbers, add *ban-me*:

ichi	1	*ichi-ban-me*	first
ni	2	*ni-ban-me*	second
san	3	*san-ban-me*	third
shi, yon	4	*yon-ban-me*	fourth
go	5	*go-ban-me*	fifth
roku	6	*roku-ban-me*	sixth
shichi, nana	7	*nana-ban-me*	seventh
hachi	8	*hachi-ban-me*	eighth
ku, kyū	9	*kyū-ban-me*	ninth
jū	10	*jū-ban-me*	tenth
jū-ichi	11	*jū-ichi-ban-me*	eleventh

and so on.

JAPANESE ADDRESSES

Note that Japanese addresses are written in exactly the opposite order than addresses in the United States. That is, the largest units come first: postal code, followed by country (*koku*), prefecture (*ken*), city (*shi, Tokyo-to, Osaka-fu*), borough (*ku*), neighborhood or ward (*chō* or *chōme*), block or street (*ban* or *banchi*), house or building number (*gō*).

Here's an example.

Nihon boeki shinkyōkai (Jetoro)
Kokusai kōryūbu

Chōsa yaku
IOKA YŪJI

〒105 Tokyo-tō, Minato-ku, Toranomon 2 chōme 2 ban 5 gō

When transcribed into roman script, as they are on letters sent to the United States or as they often appear on the reverse side of someone's name card, the units are reversed, going from smallest to largest. Also note that the name itself has been reversed, so that the given name appears first. For example:

Jetro
Japanese External Trade Organization

YŪJI IOKA
Project Manager
International Communication Department

2-2-5, Toranomon, Minato-ku, Tokyo 105, JAPAN

Alternative ways of writing this same address would be: Toranomon 2-2-5, or 2-2-5 Toranomon. The first 2 would be the *chō*, the second 2 would be the *banchi*, and the 5 would be the *gō*.

If you can't just hand the taxi driver a *meishi* or a written address, relay the information slowly and clearly, starting with the *ku* and then proceeding to the next smallest unit (unless you are going to a different town altogether, in which case you would begin with the name of the town).

HOW TO SAY "IF"

Make the conditional form of verbs by adding *ba* to the *e* stem of the verb.

taberu (tabemasu)

tabereba	if [you] eat	*Kore o **tabereba** ii n'desu.*
		You should eat this. (Literally, if you eat this, it would be good).

miru (mimasu)

mireba	if [you] see	*Sore o **mireba** ii n'desu.*
		You should see that.

kaku (kakimasu)

kakeba   if [you] write

*Tegami o **kakeba** ii n'desu.*
You should write a letter.

isogu (isogimasu)

isogeba   if [you] hurry

***Isogeba** ii n'desu.*
You should hurry.

yobu (yobimasu)

yobeba   if [you] call

***Yobeba** ii n'desu.*
You should call [him].

nomu (nomimasu)

nomeba   if [you] drink

*Mizu o **nomeba** ii n'desu.*
You should drink some
water.

shinu (shinimasu)

shineba   if [he] dies

***Shineba** ii n'desu.*
He should die.

kaeru (kaerimasu)

kaereba   if [you] return

***Kaereba** ii n'desu.*
It would be good if [she] came
back.

kau (kaimasu)

kaeba   if [you] want
to buy

***Kaeba** ii n'desu.*
You should buy it.

matsu (machimasu)

mateba   if [you] wait

***Mateba** ii n'desu.*
You should wait.

suru (shimasu)

sureba if [you] do ***Sureba** ii n'desu.*
You should do it.

kuru (kimasu)

kureba if [you] come ***Kureba** ii n'desu.*
You should come.

A phrase that ends with a conditional is often paired with another phrase, as in, if X then Y. This is a powerful combination, because now you can do things like ask directions. The pattern is as follows:

Yūbin kyoku wa, As for the post office, how
dō ikeba ii n' desu ka? should I go?

Literally, the structure of this sentence is: "As for the post office, **how should I go so it will be all right?**" In English, we would normally say something like, "How do I get to the post office?"

DOES [THE BUS] STOP HERE?

It will be useful for you to know how to ask if a bus or train stops at a certain place. The pattern to use is as follows:

NOUN + *ni tomarimasu ka?* = "Does [this bus] stop at
NOUN?"

The particle *ni* points to the place, indicated by a noun, where the verb (*tomarimasu*) occurs. Simply substitute the name of the place into this pattern.

EXERCISES

Answers are on page 54.

1. Ask where the following places are:
   a. bus stop (*basu tei*)
   b. subway station (*chikatetsu no eki*)
   c. taxi stand (*takushī noriba*)
   d. exit (*deguchi*)

2. Buy train tickets.
   a. A student (*gakusei*) ticket to Osaka, please. Special express.
   b. Two (adult) round-trip tickets (*ōfuku*) to Fukuoka. Non-smoking.
   c. Three adult (*otona*) and two children (*kodomo*), one way (*katamichi*) to Kyoto. Special express, reserved seats.
   d. One adult, one student, and two children's tickets to Kamakura, please. Special express, reserved, non-smoking.

3. Ask a taxi driver to get you to the following locations:
   a. 7-1, Nishishinjuku 2-chōme, Shinjuku-ku, Tokyo 163-07
   b. Hokkoku Shinbun, 2-5-1 Kōrinbo, Kanazawa City, Ishikawa 920, JAPAN
   c. To the station (*eki*)
   d. To the National Theater (*Kokuritsu gekijō*)

4. Ask someone how to get to the following locations:
   a. The post office (*yūbin kyoku*)
   b. Tokyo Station (*Tokyo Eki*)
   c. City Hall (*shiyakusho*)
   d. American Embassy (*Amerika Taishikan*)

5. Ask someone if a certain bus will stop at the following places in Kyoto.
   a. Kiyomizu Temple (*Kiyomizu dera*)
   b. The Kawara District (*Kawara-machi*)
   c. Nanzen Temple (*Nanzenji*)
   d. Katsura Detached Palace (*Katsura rikkyū*)

WORTH KNOWING

ABOUT TRAINS

When buying train (*densha*) tickets (*kippu*) at a ticket window (*kippu uriba*), always give your destination first. Then specify the type of ticket (round-trip, one-way). If you are a student (*gakusei*) or are traveling with children (*kodomo*), say so. Otherwise, you'll be charged for adult (*otona*) fare (*ryōkin*). Finally, give the number of the tickets you want (see page 96 for a list of numbers), and add the suffix for counting tickets (*-mai*).

There are different kinds of tickets. Everyone needs a regular passenger ticket (*jōsha-ken*), computed by the distance traveled. Additionally, if you want to travel more quickly than usual, purchase a special express ticket (*tokkyū-ken*). And if you want to reserve a seat (*zaseki*), ask for a reserved seat ticket (*shiteiseki-ken*). You can also specify a non-smoking seat (*kin'enseki*).

By far, the fastest type of rail service is the so-called Bullet Train (*Shinkansen*). One line runs along the Pacific Coast (*San'yō*) from Tokyo to Fukuoka. Another runs north from Tokyo to Morioka, and a third line, from Tokyo to Kanazawa, is presently being constructed. The ticket windows (*kippu uriba*), or the vending machines (*kenbaiki*) for the *Shinkansen* are often separated from the others. For any kind of express ticket, look for the Green Window (*midori no madoguchi*).

If you have a tourist visa, you can purchase special rail passes that are good for unlimited travel on the Japan Railways (JR) system for periods of one, two, or three weeks. These are not only very economical, but they will save you the hassle of buying tickets. Note, however, that you can't buy them in Japan. Inquire at your local travel agency before leaving home.

TAXIS AND ADDRESSES

In a city as large as Tokyo, taxi (*takushī*) drivers are hesistant to venture into unfamiliar areas. Also, during peak traffic hours, it is not uncommon for Tokyo drivers to recommend that you take the subway (*chikatetsu*) if you're going across town. In other situations, you won't have much trouble either getting a taxi or getting to where you need to be.

You can flag down taxis on the street or catch one at a taxi stop (*takushī noriba*). Just look for the red "not occupied" light on the front dash. Wait for the driver to open and close the door.

If you're staying with someone, at a hotel or an inn, or even if you're at a bus or train station, you can have someone call a taxi for you. "*Takushī o yonde itadakitai n' desu ga* (I wonder if you could call a cab for me.)"

Once you're in the cab, you can simply hand the driver a written address and ask him to take you "to this address" (*kono jūsho made*) or "to here" (*koko made*). Or using the same pattern, say the name of the place, for example "to Shinjuku Station" (*Shinjuku eki made, itte kudasai*). If you're unfamiliar with an address, it's always a good idea to have someone write it down for you.

TIPPING

There is no tipping of taxi drivers, bell hops, waiters, and such. A service charge is added to your bill whenever you eat in a hotel or when the cost of food and drink per person exceeds a certain amount. In this case, the charge is figured into the total, and all you have to do is pay the amount as it appears on your bill.

One exception to the no-tipping rule is in Japanese-style inns. If you stay in one, you will be expected to pay the maid. She assists you in many ways, such as serving you tea and sweets when you settle into your room, serving dinner and breakfast in your room, and preparing the bedding when you retire for the night.

ABOUT BUSES

In major cities, you usually pay a flat rate (*ryōkin*) for riding a bus (*basu*). If you board at the front of the bus you'll likely have to pay when you get on. If you board the bus at the rear door, you'll pay when you get off.

Don't panic if you don't have the right change (*o-tsuri*). You can slip a 1,000 yen bill into the coin changer next to the driver's seat. A 100-yen coin can also be broken into 10 yen coins. Drop the appropriate coins into the slot. Otherwise, you can break a bill at a store by saying, "*Kuzushite kudasaimasu ka*? (Could you break this, please?)"

In smaller cities and rural areas, you usually pay according to the distance traveled. As you board, look for a machine that automatically dispenses a ticket with a number on it. Take the ticket, and hand it over with your fare when you get off. The display at the front of the bus will tell you how much to pay. If no ticket pops out of the dispenser, that means you'll be paying full fare.

As for getting off at the right place, there are several strategies. One is to listen carefully for the stop as it is announced (once as you leave the stop just prior to yours, and then again when the bus approaches your stop). If you're not confident about doing this, then there's nothing wrong with asking the driver (or someone else on the bus) to let you know when the bus reaches your stop.

"Sumimasen. (Your destination) ni oritai n' desu ga, oshiete kudasaimasu ka? (Excuse me. I'd like to get off at . . . Could you please let me know when we get there?)"

ADDITIONAL VOCABULARY

annaijo	information booth
aruku (arukimasu)	to walk
baiten	kiosk
chizu	map
eki	train station
futsū, kakueiki teisha	regular train (stops at all stations)
genzaichi	where you are now (on a map)
gurīnsha	first class (green car)
gakusei	student
hidari ni magaru	turn left
hodōkyō	pedestrian overpass
jōshaken	regular railway ticket (cost determined by mileage)
kado	street corner
kaisoku densha	rapid-service train (stops infrequently)
kenbaiki	automated ticket machines
kin'en seki	non-smoking seat
kōban	police box
koin rokkā	coin locker
kōsaten	intersection
kyūkō	express train
massugu	straight ahead
michi, dōri	street
midori no madoguchi	window for express tickets
migi ni magaru	turn right
nimotsu azukarijo	luggage check-in

odan hodō	pedestrian crossing
otona	adult
shitei seki	reserved seat
tokkyūken	express ticket

ANSWERS TO EXERCISES

1. a. *Basu tei wa, doko desu ka?*
   b. *Chikatetsu no eki wa, doko desu ka?*
   c. *Takushī noriba wa doko desu ka?*
   d. *Deguchi wa, doko desu ka?*
2. a. *Osaka made, gakusei, ichi-mai kudasai. Tokkyū ken mo onegai shimasu.* b. *Fukuoka, ōfuku, ni-mai. Kin'en seki o onegai shimasu.* c. *Kyoto made, katamichi, otona, san-mai; kodomo, ni-mai. Tokkyū ken no shitei seki, o onegai shimasu.* d. *Kamakura made, otona, ichimai; gakusei, ichi-mai; kodomo ni-mai kudasai. Tokkyū ken no kin'en seki o onegai shimasu.*
3. a. *Shinjuku-ku, Nishishinjuku ni no nana no ichi made, itte kudasai.* b. *Korinbo, ni no go no ichi made, itte kudasai.* c. *Eki made, itte kudasai.* d. *Kokuritsu gekijō made, itte kudasai.*
4. a. *Yūbin kyoku wa, dō ikeba ii n'desu ka?*
   b. *Tokyo Eki wa, dō ikeba ii n'desu ka?*
   c. *Shiyakusho wa, dō ikeba ii n'desu ka?*
   d. *Amerika Taishikan wa, dō ikeba ii n'desu ka?*
5. a. *Kono basu wa, Kiyomizu dera ni tomarimasu ka?*
   b. *Kono basu wa, Kawara-machi ni tomarimasu ka?*
   c. *Kono basu wa, Nanzenji ni tomarimasu ka?*
   d. *Kono basu wa, Katsura rikkyū ni tomarimasu ka?*

4 EATING OUT

(Noun) o hitotsu, onegai shimasu.	I'll have a . . .
Sō shimashō.	Let's do that.
(Noun) ga suki desu.	I like . . .
Daijōbu desu.	It's okay.
Jā, sore ni shimashō.	I'll have that.
(Noun) no hō ga ii n'desu.	I prefer . . .
(Go)chisō-sama deshita.	Thanks for a delicious meal.
Nani ga arimasu ka?	What do you have?

ORDERING COFFEE

WAITER **Irasshaimase. Nani ni nasaimasu ka?**
(Welcome. What will you have?)

CUSTOMER **Kōhī o futatsu to kōra o hitotsu onegai shimasu.** (Two coffees and a cola, please.)

WAITER   **Hai, kashikomarimashita. Shōshō omachi kudasai.** (Yes, I understand. It'll just take a minute.)

Word List

Irasshaimase.	Come in, welcome. (Honorific, imperative form of *kuru*)
kōhī	coffee
shōshō	a little while
omachi kudasai	please wait (an honorific, imperative form of *matsu*)

DECIDING ON A RESTAURANT

HOST   **Shokuji o shimashō ka?** (Shall we have dinner?)

GUEST   **Sō shimashō.** (Yes, let's do that.)

HOST   **Nani ga ii ka nē. Nihon ryōri? Chūka ryōri?** (What would be good, I wonder. Japanese food? Chinese food?)

GUEST   **Nihon ryōri ga suki desu nē.** (Japanese food sounds good.)

HOST   **Sakana wa?** (What about fish?)

GUEST   **Daijōbu desu.** (Okay. No problem.)

HOST   **(O)sashimi mo taberaremasu ka?** (Can you eat raw fish?)

GUEST   **Ee, daisuki desu.** (Yes. I love it.)

HOST   **Jā, sushiya e ikimashō.** (So, let's go to a sushi shop.)

Word List

shokuji	a meal
ka ne	[I] wonder (particles: *ka* indicates a question, *nē* seeks affirmation)
Nihon ryōri	Japanese cuisine
Chūka ryōri	Chinese cuisine

sakana	fish
daisuki	a favorite [of mine]
ee	yes
(o)sashimi	raw fish (o is an honorific prefix)
mo	also (particle: indicates inclusion)
taberaremasu	can eat (polite, potential form of *taberu*)
sushiya	a sushi shop
e	to (particle: indicates movement toward some point)
ikimashō	let's go (polite, suggestive form of *iku*)

IN A RESTAURANT

HOST **Koko no tenpura wa oishii desu yo.** (The tempura here is good.)

GUEST **Jā, sore ni shimashō.** (So let's have that.)

HOST **(O)nomimono wa? (O)sake? Bīru?** (What would you like to drink? Sake? Beer?)

GUEST **(O)sake no hō ga ii n'desu.** (I prefer sake.)

HOST **Sumimasen. (O)kanjō o onegai shimasu.** (Excuse me. The bill, please.)

WAITER **Kashikomarimashita.** (Right away.)

GUEST **Gochisō-sama deshita.** (Thanks for a wonderful meal.)

HOST **Iie. Dō itashimashite.** (Not at all. Don't mention it.)

Word List

tenpura	tempura
oishii	tasty
(o)nomimono	a drink (*o* is an honorific prefix)
(o)sake	rice wine (*o* is an honorific prefix)
bīru	beer
(o)kanjō	the bill (*o* is an honorific prefix)

ORDERING A DRINK

WAITER	**Irasshaimase.** (Welcome.)
CUSTOMER	**Bīru wa nani ga arimasu ka?** (What kind of beer do you have?)
WAITER	**Asahi to Kirin to Sapporo ga arimasu.** (Asahi, Kirin, and Sapporo.)
CUSTOMER	**Jā, Asahi o ni-hon to gurasu wain o ip-pai onegai shimasu.** (I see. Give me two Asahis and two glasses of wine, please.)
WAITER	**Wain wa, aka desu ka, shiro desu ka?** (Red? Or white?)
CUSTOMER	**Aka o onegai shimasu.** (Red please.)

Word List

Asahi, Kirin, Sapporo	popular brands of Japanese beer
ni-hon	two bottles (*hon* is a counter for cylindrical objects)
gurasu wain	wine (sold by the glass)
ip-pai	two glasses (*hai* is a counter for cups of liquid)
aka	red (noun)
shiro	white (noun)

EXPLANATIONS

LET'S DO THAT

You can make a suggestion by changing *shimasu* to *shimashō*. The conjugation is simple. Just change *-masu* to *-mashō*. As in:

tabemasu	to eat
tabemashō	let's eat

mimasu	to see
mimashō	let's see
kakimasu	to write
kakimashō	let's write
isogimasu	to hurry
isogimashō	let's hurry
yobimasu	to call
yobimashō	let's call
nomimasu	to drink
nomimashō	let's drink
shinimasu	to die
shinimashō	let's die
kaerimasu	to return
kaerimashō	let's return
kaimasu	to buy
kaimashō	let's buy
machimasu	to wait
machimashō	let's wait
shimasu	to do
shimashō	let's do

. . . . IS BETTER

You'll want to be able to express a preference. You can do this by saying that something is better than another alternative. The pattern is as follows.

NOUN + *no hō ga ii desu* = "I prefer NOUN."

For example, *(O)sake no hō ga ii n'desu.* You'd rather have sake than beer or some other possibility.

WHAT DO YOU HAVE?

You can inquire about which kinds of things a shop might have by using the sentence "*Nani ga arimasu ka?* (What do you have?)" You might want to narrow things down a bit by first mentioning a topic, and then adding the phrase. Remember that the particle *wa* marks a topic, and the particle *ga* marks the subject.

Bīru wa, nani ga arimasu ka?   As for beer, what do you have?

If you have something specifically in mind, you can ask about it by using this same pattern without a topic. For example, *Kirin bīru ga arimasu ka?* (Do you have Kirin beer?)

Note that the verb *arimasu* is used to indicate the presence or non-presence (*arimasen*) of inanimate things. For animate things, use *imasu* or *imasen*.

Inanimate
Arimasu   Kirin bīru ga arimasu.   There is Kirin beer.

Animate
Imasu   Nihonjin ga imasu.   There are Japanese [here].

EXERCISES

Answers are on page 65.

1. You're in a coffee shop. Ask for the following items:
   a. one coffee and two cups of tea
   b. one cola and three cups of coffee
   c. Japanese tea
   d. one coffee and a piece of cake (*keiki*)

2. Suggest to your partner that you do the following:
   a. have dinner together
   b. have sashimi
   c. go to a sushi shop
   d. drink beer

3. Given two alternatives, express your preference for the first.
   a. sushi, sashimi
   b. sake, beer
   c. coffee, Japanese tea
   d. tempura, teriyaki

4. Inquire to see if the restaurant you have entered has the following items:
   a. sukiyaki
   b. tempura
   c. noodles (*udon, soba* or *rāmen*)
   d. curry rice (*kare raisu*)

WORTH KNOWING

COFFEE SHOPS

Because urban housing is crowded and entertaining at home is difficult, people often gather at the many coffee shops (*kissaten*), which dot the landscape. Each shop has its own personality—some play jazz, others play only classical music, some display pottery, and so forth. But they all serve about the same things: coffee, tea, soft drinks, ice cream, cakes, and such. Many of them also serve snacks and light dishes such as sandwiches, spaghetti, pancakes, and fried rice.

WHO PAYS THE BILL?

If someone suggests you go out for dinner, that person is the one who usually pays the bill, especially if he or she says "*shōtai shimasu* (invite you)" or "*ogotte agemasu* (treat you)." When everyone pays his or her own, it's called *warikan*. Rather than suggesting the bill be split, however, reciprocating on another occasion (such as when your host visits you) is more appropriate. Generally speaking, the less money is made an issue, the better it is. Show your appreciation by letting your hosts know how much you enjoyed their hospitality. Saying *Gochisō-sama deshita* after a meal is a must.

ASKING FOR THE CHECK

At most restaurants, the check is called *(o)kanjō*. Ask for it by saying, *(O)kanjō o kudasai.* There are exceptions. If you're eating at a sushi shop, the correct term is *(o)aisō*.

KNOW YOUR NOODLES

One of the great things about Japan is the wide variety of noodles that are available. *Soba* are brownish, buckwheat noodles. *Udon* are larger, white noodles. *Rāmen* are a Japanese version of Chinese noodles. And Western *supagettī* is also popular, served with a wide variety of sauces, including fish eggs. The adaptation of foreign foods is pretty fascinating. You can even get spaghetti sandwiches!

NIGHT LIFE

When enjoying an evening out, it is customary to move from shop to shop—eating some special dish at one restaurant, then moving on to another. As the night grows deeper, the focus shifts from food to drink, and inevitably you will find yourself at a bar that your host frequents. Walking into a bar unannounced is not unheard of. But it is always better to go with someone who is known to the management.

Each bar has its own style. Some are quiet, some are not. Most have elaborate video *karaoke* machines to help you pass the time. It's hard to get out of singing a tune or two since the laser disk and tape selections usually contain various hits in English: "Yesterday," "I Did It My Way," and so forth. Needless to say, making a fool out of yourself is a *great* way to make friends.

Compared to bars in the United States, the options are rather limited: beer, sake, and whiskey (usually mixed with water and called *mizuwari*) are the regular drinks served. The variety of non–alcoholic beverages is even more limited. You can always ask for a *jūsu*, orange soda.

ADDITIONAL VOCABULARY

DESSERTS AND LIGHT FARE

aisu kurīmu	ice cream
hotto keiki	pancakes
sandoitchi	sandwich

DRINKS

miruku, gyūnyū	milk
hotto miruku	hot milk
kōcha	black tea
kokoa	hot chocolate
mizu	water
nama-bīru	draft beer
(o)cha	Japanese (green) tea
(o)hiya	cold water
orenji jūsu	orange juice
sōda	soda

MAIN FARE

donburi	cooked rice topped with various vegetables and meat:
• **oyako**	• chicken and eggs (literally, parents and children) on rice
• **unagi**	• broiled marinated eels on rice
(go)han	cooked rice, a meal

misoshiru	miso soup
mizutaki	chicken simmered in broth (usually cooked at your table)
nigirizushi	bite-sized bits of cooked, vinegared rice topped with fresh seafood:
• **awabi**	• abalone
• **ebi**	• shrimp
• **ika**	• squid
• **ikura**	• salmon roe
• **maguro**	• tuna
• **tako**	• octopus
• **toro**	• the fatty belly flesh of a tuna
• **uni**	• sea urchin
norimaki	cooked rice with vegetables wrapped in seaweed (*nori*)
rāmen	Chinese-style noodles
shabushabu	beef simmered in broth
soba	buckwheat noodles
supagettī	spaghetti
teishoku	a fixed menu
tonkatsu	pork cutlet
udon	thick white noodles
kitsune udon	noodles with fried *tōfu* (bean curd)
tenpura udon	noodles with tempura
yakitori	charcoal-grilled chicken, chicken liver, and green onions on a bamboo stick

GENERAL TERMS

washoku	Japanese cuisine
yōshoku	Western cuisine

ANSWERS TO EXERCISES

1. a. *Kōhī o hitotsu to kōcha o futatsu onegai shimasu.* b. *Kōra o hitotsu to kōhī o mitsu onegai shimasu.* c. *Ocha o onegai shimasu.* d. *Kōhī o hitotsu to keiki o hitotsu onegai shimasu.*
2. a. *Shokuji o shimashō.* b. *Sashimi o tabemashō.* c. *Sushiya e ikimashō.* d. *Bīru o nomimashō.*
3. a. *(O)sushi no hō ga ii desu.* b. *(O)sake no hō ga ii desu.* c. *Kōhī no hō ga ii desu.* d. *Tenpura no hō ga ii desu.*
4. a. *Sukiyaki ga arimasu ka?* b. *Tenpura ga arimasu ka?* c. *Udon/soba ga arimasu ka?* d. *Kare raisu ga arimasu ka?*

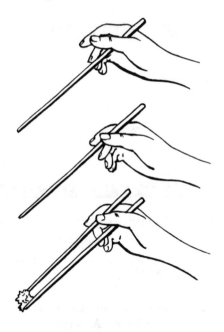

Hold the bottom chopstick stationary. Hold the top chopstick with your index and middle fingers. Without moving your thumb, raise and lower only the upper chopstick.

5 DOING BUSINESS

KEY WORDS AND PHRASES

Hajimemashite. Sumisu desu.	Pleased to meet you. I'm Smith.
Tsumaranai mono desu ga, dōzo	This is nothing much, but please . . . .
Kyōshuku desu.	[I'm] truly grateful.
(O)sewa ni narimashita.	I'm indebted to your kindness.
De wa, shitsurei shimasu.	Well, then, I guess I'll be going.

CONVERSATIONS

BEING INTRODUCED AND EXCHANGING
BUSINESS CARDS

TANAKA **Sumisu-san, uchi no shachō o (go)shōkai shimasu.** (Mr. Smith, let me introduce our president to you.)

SMITH **Zehi onegai shimasu.** (By all means. Please do.)

TANAKA **Shachō, kochira wa Amerika no Sumisu desu.** (President, this is Mr. Smith from the United States.)

SMITH   [Bowing.] **Hajimemashite.** (Pleased to meet
          you.) **Sumisu desu.** (I'm Smith.) [Handing a
          name card to Tanaka-san] **Dōzo.** (My card.)
SATŌ   **Dōmo, a, Noberu no kata desu ne.
          Hajimemashite. Mitsubishi no Satō desu.
          Dōzo.** (Thank you. Ah, you're from Novell, I see.
          Pleased to meet you. I'm Satō of Mitsubishi
          Corporation.)
SMITH   [Taking Sato's name card with two hands.]
          Arigatō gozaimasu. (Thank you.)

Word List

uchi no	our
shachō	company president
(go)shōkai shimasu	to introduce (polite, honorific form of *shōkai suru*)
zehi	by all means
kochira	this person [here]
Amerika no Sumisu.	Smith from America.
dōmo	Thanks (shortened verion of *domō arigatō gozaimasu*)
a	ah
Noberu	Novell
kata	person (honorific)
Mitsubishi	Mitsubishi

GIVING A GIFT

SMITH   **Tsumaranai mono desu ga, dōzo.** (This is
          really nothing, but please . . . .)
SATŌ   **Dōmo, hontō ni arigatō gozaimasu.
          (O)kizukai itadaite, sumimasen.** (Thank you
          very much. You didn't need to do that.)
SMITH   **Amerika no shashin-shū desu.** (It's a photo
          album of the United States.)

SATŌ **Kirei desu nē. Kyōshuku desu.** (These are very nice. I'm honored.)

Word List

mono	thing
ga	but
ki o tsukatte itadaite	you're being so considerate (*-te* form of *ki o tsukau* + *-te* form of *itadaku*)
shashin-shū	photography collection
kirei	nice, pretty

THANKING SOMEONE AND ASKING FOR CONTINUED COOPERATION

SMITH **Iroiro, (o)sewa ni narimashita.** (Thanks for all you've done.)

SATŌ **Kochira koso.** (Thank you for what you've done.)

SMITH **Kore kara mo, yoroshiku onegai shimasu.** (Here's to the future.)

SATŌ **Kochira koso. Yoroshiku onegai shimasu.** (My sentiments exactly. To the future.)

Word List

iroiro	various, in many ways
(o)sewa ni narimashita	I've become indebted to your kindness.
kochira koso	my sentiments, exactly
kore kara mo	from now on (as before)

TAKING LEAVE

SMITH **Kyō wa, hontō ni arigatō gozaimashita.** (Thank you very much. It's been quite a day.)

SATŌ **Dō itashimashite.** (Not at all.)

SMITH **Mata, chikai uchi ni aimashō.** (I'm looking forward to meeting again soon.)

SATŌ	**Ee, sō shimashō.** (Yes, let's do that.)
SMITH	**De wa, shitsurei shimasu.** (Well, then, I guess I'll be going.)

Word List

chikai uchi ni	before too long
mata	again
aimashō	let's meet (polite, suggestive form of *au*)
de wa	well then

EXPLANATIONS

UCHI

The term *uchi* or "inner," refers to that which lies within one's own circle. *Uchi no shachō,* then, means "our president." You could say, for instance, *uchi no musume,* "our daughter." The opposite of *uchi* is *soto,* as in the famous saying, *"Fuku wa uchi! Oni wa soto!* (In with prosperity! Out with the devil!)"

Strong group consciousness is a cliche of Japanese culture. But it is often the case that some Japanese strongly identify with a larger group. This is why Satō refers to himself, at least in a business setting, as *"Mitsubishi no Satō desu* (Satō of Mitsubishi)."

SELF DEPRECATION

It is best to be modest about oneself and those things in one's own private circle. It's bad form to brag (unless in joking) about one's accomplishments or one's own family members. This is why the gift that you give someone else is *tsumaranai* (of little value or interest) or *nani mo nai* (nothing much).

WHO'S WHO IN A JAPANESE COMPANY

The hierarchy at a Japanese company is to be taken seriously. Some visitors to Japan make the mistake of not knowing who has the authority to make decisions and who does not. For instance, the one who speaks the best English or seems the most communicative is rarely the one who deserves the greatest deference. Do your research beforehand, and take a careful look at the *meishi* (name cards) you receive when introduced to someone.

kaichō	chairman
shachō	chief executive officer, president
fuku-shachō	executive vice-president
senmu	senior managing director
jōmu	managing director
buchō	director
jichō	senior manager
kachō	manager
shunin, kakarichō	supervisor

A senior managing director, managing director, and, in a large corporation, even a director may have the authority of a vice-president in a U.S. company. The word *torishimariyaku* before the title means that the person is a board member.

USING VERBS TO EXPRESS DESIRE

Itadakitai is the desiderative form of *itadaku*. Using this desiderative, or *-tai* form, you can say that you want to do a certain action, such as, I want to go, I want to eat, and so forth. It conjugates like the polite *-masu* form that you already know. Instead of *-masu*, add *-tai* to the noun-forming stem of the verb. To make it more polite, add *n'desu* to the end of the sentence.

taberu (tabemasu)

tabetai   want to eat   *Sushi ga **tabetai** n'desu.*
[I] want to eat sushi.

miru (mimasu)

mitai   want to see   *Eiga ga **mitai** n'desu.*
[I] want to see a movie.

kaku (kakimasu)

kakitai   want to write   *Tegami o **kakitai** n'desu.*
[I] want to write a letter.

isogu (isogimasu)

isogitai   want to hurry   ***Isogitai** n'desu.*
[I] want to hurry.

yobu (yobimasu)

yobitai   want to call   *Tanaka-san o **yobitai** n'desu.*
[I] want to call Mr. Tanaka.

nomu (nomimasu)

nomitai   want to drink   *Bīru ga **yomitai** n'desu.*
[I] want to drink beer.

shinu (shinimasu)

shinitai   want to die   ***Shinitai** n'desu.*
[I] want to die.

kaeru (kaerimasu)

kaeritai   want to return   *Sugu **kaeritai** n'desu.*
[I] want to return right away.

kau (kaimasu)

kaitai	want to buy	*Hon ga **kaitai** n'desu.*
		[I] want to buy a book.

matsu (machimasu)

machitai	want to wait	*Shichiji made **machitai** n'desu.*
		[I] want to wait until seven o'clock.

suru (shimasu)

shitai	want to do	*Benkyō **shitai** n'desu.*
		[I] want to study.

kuru (kimasu)

kitai	want to come	*Tanaka-san mo **kitai** n'desu.*
		Mrs. Tanaka wants to come, too.

PRONOUNS

The three most common pronouns are *mono, koto,* and *no.*

All can be translated as "things." But their usage is different. *Mono* is used for concrete things (including persons), and *koto* is used for abstract things. You would say *tsumaranai mono* (something of little value) about some tangible object. A *tsumaranai koto* might be a not-so-great thing to say.

The pronoun *no* is the most flexible of all because it can be used for either concrete or abstract things.

Note that modifiers come before pronouns. Common modifiers are adjectives, as in *takai mono* (something expensive), or verbs, as in *ageru mono* (something given). If you don't know the specific name of something, you can often get by with describing it with adjectives and verbs and adding the correct pronoun at the end. For example, *tabetai mono* (what I want to eat), *shitai koto* (what I want to do), and so forth.

EXERCISES

Answers are on page 77.

1. Introduce the following people:
   a. your company's president
   b. your company's vice-president
   c. your company's senior managing director
   d. your company's managing director

2. Present the following gifts:
   a. just a little something
   b. a book of photographs of America
   c. [something] from our company
   d. a memento (*(o)miyage*) from Hawaii.

3. You'd like to thank your business partners
   a. for all the things they've done for you.
   b. for the day's activities.
   c. for taking you out to eat the day before (*kinō*).

4. At the end of your meeting, tell your business partner
   a. that you're looking forward to meeting again soon.
   b. that you'll have to be going.

WORTH KNOWING

EXCHANGING NAME CARDS
Be sure to take an ample supply of name cards or *meishi* when you go to Japan. You'll be exchanging these whenever

you meet someone, and they will remain behind to become an important means of contact. These cards provide vital information: not only the name and address of the person, but the status of that person as well. The Japanese rely on these cards to determine the appropriate level of speech for each social situation, to whom certain questions should be addressed, and so forth.

When you meet someone, offer your *meishi* by turning it around so it will be readable to the person receiving it and holding it out in front of you with one hand. When you receive a *meishi,* hold it with both hands, and take a moment to look at it carefully. Say the name out loud— *Satō-san desu ne*—and ask for their favor—*Dōzo yoroshiku onegai shimasu.*

Once you're seating around a table, it is acceptable to lay the cards out before you for easy reference.

BOWING OR SHAKING HANDS

"When in Rome do as the Romans do." The Japanese version of this maxim is *Gō ni itte wa, gō ni shitagae.* (When you go to a village, do as the villagers do.) But this is easier said than done.

The customs of bowing and hand shaking are good examples of how hard it actually is to follow the villager's lead. When you bow, bow like a pine tree rather than a willow. That is, try to keep your back straight. Your head should come forward, eyes focused down, but don't overdo it. Most of the movement comes at the hips, rather than along your spine or neck. Slide your hands down your thighs toward your knees. The deeper the bow, the more humble. It's a good idea to watch your partner and to bow as deeply as he or she does.

Shaking hands is now fairly common in Japan. But don't expect a firm grip. Many Japanese still hold out their hands limply and let that pass for a handshake.

GIFT GIVING

Gift giving has always been an important part of Japanese social custom. Gifts are often exchanged during social interactions, such as meeting with a client. In some situations, especially when important business is transacted, it is better to wait until just before one leaves to give a gift.

What to give? Here are some suggestions for appropriate gifts:

For an important client	Books, ornaments, china, liquor, or some practical item of high quality and good design. Something from your home country is a good idea.
When visiting someone's home	Flowers, fruit, wine.
Making a request	A small box of candy or confections.

DECISION MAKING

U.S. business people might prefer to conduct negotiations with their counterparts in small, private meetings. But because decisions tend to be made by consensus in Japan, they involve all those affected; one-to-one meetings are rare. In fact, you know you're being taken seriously when the group that has gathered is a large one, with representatives from numerous divisions of the company present. Even a president or owner of a company will hesitate to make quick decisions for the entire group.

Because of this process of gathering consensus, it may take a long time before you get the answer you want. If someone tells you, *Sore wa ii kangae desu ne.* (That's a good idea.), it actually means you're still a long way from an agreement. If they say, *Ii henji ga dekiru yō ni ganbarimasu,* (We'll do our best to give you a favorable reply), you know you're about ready to close a deal.

Above all, work to establish a relationship of trust. Developing personal ties with your business associates is crucial.

ADDITIONAL VOCABULARY

aisatsu	courtesy call
akaji	debt, deficit, in the red
bōeki masatsu	trade dispute
gijutsu	technology
ginkō	bank
hinshitsu	quality
hisho	secretary
kabu	stock
kabushiki gaisha	corporation
kaigi	meeting
kawase rēto	exchange rate
keiei	management
keiyakusho	contract
kōjō	factory
konki	this fiscal year
kōshō	negotiations
kosuto	cost
kuroji	surplus, profit, in the black
mitsumori	estimate
nagai tsukiai	long-standing relationship
nebiki suru	to discount
(o)kane	money
patento, tokkyo	patent
raiki	next fiscal year
ryūtsū	distribution
setsubi tōshi	capital spending
shakkin	loan

shihon	capital
torihiki	business, transactions, dealings
tōshi	investment
unsō	shipping
zaiko	inventory, stock
zeikin	tax
zenki	previous fiscal year

ANSWERS TO EXERCISES

1. a. *Kochira wa uchi no shachō desu.*
   b. *Kochira wa uchi no fuku-shachō desu.*
   c. *Kochira wa uchi no senmu desu.*
   d. *Kochira wa uchi no jōmu desu.*
2. a. *Tsumaranai mono desu ga, dōzo.*
   b. *Amerika no shashinshū desu ga, dōzo.*
   c. *Uchi no kaisha kara desu ga, dōzo.*
   d. *Hawaii kara no omiyage desu ga, dōzo.*
3. a. *Iroiro, osewa ni narimashita.*
   b. *Kyō wa, hontō ni arigatō gozaimashita.*
   c. *Kinō wa gochisō-sama deshita.*
4. a. *Chikai uchi ni, aimashō.*
   b. *De wa, shitsurei shimasu.*

6 SHOPPING

KEY WORDS AND PHRASES

Kore o kudasai.	Please give me this one.
Mittsu kudasai.	Please give me three.
Sore o misete kudasai.	Please show me that one.
Motto ōkii no o misete kudasai.	Please show me a bigger one.
Kōkūbin de onegai shimasu.	By airmail, please.
Mantan ni shite kudasai.	Fill it up with gas, please.

CONVERSATIONS

BUYING BY WEIGHT

SHOPKEEPER	**Irasshaimase.** (Welcome.)
CUSTOMER	**Kore o, ni-hyaku guramu kudasai.** (Could I have 200 grams of this, please.)
SHOPKEEPER	**Hai, kashikomarimashita.** (Got it.)
CUSTOMER	**Ikura desu ka?** (How much is it?)
SHOPKEEPER	**Rop-pyaku yon-jū en desu.** (640 yen.)

Word List

ni-hyaku	200
guramu	gram
rop-pyaku	600
yon-jū	40
en	yen

BUYING BY NUMBER

SHOPKEEPER **Irasshaimase.** (Welcome.)

CUSTOMER **Kono (o)manjū wa, ikura desu ka?** (How much are these Japanese cakes?)

SHOPKEEPER **Hitotsu, hyaku go-jū en desu.** (150 yen for one.)

CUSTOMER **Mittsu kudasai.** (Could I have three, please.)

SHOPKEEPER **Arigatō gozaimasu.** (Thank you.)

Word List

(o) manjū	a Japanese confection filled with bean-jam
hyaku	100
go-jū	50
mittsu	three

ASKING A SALESPERSON TO SHOW AN ITEM

SALESPERSON **Irasshaimase.** (Welcome.)

CUSTOMER **Sore o misete kudasai.** (Could you show me that one, please?)

SALESPERSON **Kore desu ka?** (This one?)

CUSTOMER **Hai, sō desu.** (Yes. That's it.)

SALESPERSON [Handing the item to the customer] **Hai, dōzo.** (Here you go.)

Word List

misete kudasai	please show (*te* form of *miseru* + *kudasai*)
sō desu	that's right, that's so
dōzo	please [go ahead and take a look]

FINDING THE CORRECT SIZE

CUSTOMER **Emu-saizu o misete kudasai.** (Could I see this in a medium?)

SALESPERSON [Handing the item to the customer] **Hai, dōzo. Ikaga desu ka?** (Yes, here you are. How do you like it?)

CUSTOMER **Chotto chīsai desu. Motto ōkii no o misete kudasai.** (It's a little small. Could you show me a larger one?)

SALESPERSON [Handing another item to the customer] **Eru-saizu desu. Dōzo. Ikaga desu ka?** (This is a large. Please. How's that?)

CUSTOMER **Chōdo ii desu. Ikura desu ka?** (Just right. How much is it?)

SALESPERSON **Go-sen hap-pyaku en desu.** (5,800 yen.)

CUSTOMER **Jā, kore ni shimashō.** (Then, I'll take this.)

SALESPERSON **Dōmo arigatō gozaimasu.** (Thank you very much.)

Word List

emu-saizu	medium size
Ikaga desu ka?	How do you like it?
chotto chīsai	a little small
motto ōkii	a little bigger
eru-saizu	large size
chōdo ii	just right
go-sen hap-pyaku en	5,800 yen

AT THE POST OFFICE

CUSTOMER [Handing a letter to the clerk] **Kore wa ikura desu ka?** (How much is this?)

CLERK **Kōkūbin desu ka, funabin desu ka?** (Air mail or surface mail?)

CUSTOMER **Kōkūbin de onegai shimasu.** (Air mail, please.)

CLERK **Hyaku go-jū en desu.** (That will be 150 yen.)

Word List

kōkūbin	airmail
funabin	surface mail
de	by (particle: indicates the means by which something is done)

AT A GAS STATION

CUSTOMER **Mantan ni shite kudasai.** (Fill it up, please.)

ATTENDANT **Hai, kashikomarimashita.** (Yes, I understand.)

Word List

mantan	full tank

EXPLANATIONS

LOAN WORDS

Not infrequently, visitors to Japan are thrown by English words pronounced as Japanese. You might not suspect that *emu saizu* is medium size and *eru saizu* means a large. On the other hand, the Japanese might think it odd if you don't understand the words since they are, after all, English. The problem is pronunciation. Japanese has fewer sounds than English; morever, there is little sliding from one sound to another. So table becomes *teburu*, tunnel becomes *tonneru*, and virus becomes *buirusu*. It takes a little getting used to.

The good news is that most Japanese have studied English, and this can work to your advantage. Just remember: you must not only recognize English words as they say them, but you must also pronounce them as they do. If you can stay within the Japanese sound system, and if you resist the temptation to blend one sound into another, you'll be miles ahead of your peers! For a list of possible Japanese sounds, refer to pages 93–96.

USING *I*-TYPE ADJECTIVES WITH *NO*, THE PRONOUN

One way to specify something whose name you don't know is to use the pronoun *no* with an adjective of size, color, and so on. Note that *i-*type adjectives (or those adjectives that end in *i*) precede the word they modify. For example,

akai no	red one
aoi no	blue one
atsui no	hot one
chīsai no	small one
motto chīsai no	a smaller one
ōkii no	big one
motto ōkii no	a bigger one
tsumetai no	cold one

GETTING THE RIGHT FIT

You'll want to be able to express various degrees of fit. Here are the words that will let you do it.

motto	more	*motto ōkii*	bigger
chotto	a little bit	*chotto ōkii*	a bit too big
chōdo	exactly	*chōdo ii*	just right

PRESENTING ALTERNATIVES

You already know that questions are made by adding *ka* to the end of a sentence. If you want to present or ask for alternatives, try combining two short interrogative sentences. The pattern is as follows:

. . . desu ka, . . . desu ka?

You can insert many different types of words, such as the following:

NOUNS	*Kōkūbin* **desu ka,** *funabin* **desu ka?**	Air mail or surface mail?
PRONOUNS	*Watakushi* **desu ka,** *anata* **desu ka?**	You or I?
ADJECTIVES	*Ōkii* **desu ka,** *chīsai* **desu ka?**	Big or small?
VERBS	*Taberu n'***desu ka,** *nomu n'***desu ka?**	Are you going to eat or drink?

In the last pattern, the verb is nominalized by the *no* which follows. Here it is contracted to *n'*.

EXERCISES

Answers are on page 89.

1. Try pronouncing these English words as the Japanese would.
   a. bargain
   b. gallery   (as in art gallery)
   b. convenience store
   c. supermarket

2. You're at a store buying candy, which is sold by weight. Please ask for the following amounts.
   a. 10 grams
   b. 90 grams
   c. 200 grams
   d. 250 grams

3. You're buying souvenirs at a street market. Ask the vendor for the following numbers of the item.
   a. one
   b. three
   c. five
   d. seven

4. You're at a shoe store on the Ginza. Ask the salesperson if you could have a look at a few pairs.
   a. the ones in your hands
   b. those near you
   c. those far from you

5. Using adjectives followed by *no*, ask a salesperson to show you the following items.
   a. a red one
   b. a blue one
   c. a small one
   d   a smaller one
   e. a big one
   f. a bigger one

WORTH KNOWING

SOME SHOPPING TIPS

Most stores open at about 10:00 A.M. but close at different times according to type. Department stores and supermarkets shut their doors around 6:30, while smaller neighborhood stores might stay open until 9:00 P.M. or later. Many convenience stores, now plentiful in the cities, often stay open twenty-four hours a day. Sunday is a regular shopping day for big stores, which have their day off sometime during the week.

Prices for items are usually not negotiable. The exceptions are at flea markets (*nomi no ichi*), secondhand shops (*shichiya*), and large electronics and camera stores (as found in Tokyo's Akihabara district). If you're courageous, you might ask someone to give you a break: *Yasuku shite moraimasu ka?*

Most stores do not have the space for a large inventory. But you can have things ordered—*Chūmon shite kudasaimasu ka?*—if you're willing to wait.

Most stores will let you try on clothes. Exchanges are also acceptable, provided you show a receipt. If you buy something that is defective, don't hesistate to take it back. In Japan, the customer rules, and few questions are asked. Generally speaking, you can expect both quality and service.

METRIC SYSTEM

The metric system is used in measuring length, weight, volume, and temperature in Japan. Important measure words include the following:

guramu	gram (g)
kiro, kiroguramu	kilogram (kg)
rittoru	liter (l)
senchi, senchimētoru	centimeter (c)
mētoru	meter (m)
kiro, kiromētoru	kilometer (km)
sesshi	Centigrade (C)
kashi	Fahrenheit (F)

Metric equivalents are as follows.

Metric	English		English	Metric
1 kg	2.2 lb		1 lb	450 g
1 l	0.26 gal (U.S.)		1 gal	4.5 l
1 cm	0.39 in.		1 in	2.5 cm
1 m	3.3 ft		1 ft	30 cm
1 km	0.62 mile		1 mile	1.6 km
0°C	32°F			
100°C	212°F			

COLOR, SIZE, AND DEGREE TERMS (ADJECTIVES)

akai	red
aoi	blue, green
amai	sweet
atsui	hot
chīsai	small
hikui	low
karai	salty, spicy
karui	light
kiiroi	yellow
kitsui	tight, arduous
kuroi	black
mijikai	short
nagai	long
nigai	bitter
ōkii	big
omoi	heavy
samui	cold [weather]
shiroi	white
takai	tall, expensive
tsumetai	cold [liquid]
yasui	cheap
yurui	loose

JAPANESE CURRENCY

The Japanese unit of currency is actually *en* rather than *yen*. The English loan word *yen* is a prewar romanization of the same word. The romanized *e* sound was once written *ye,* as in the surnames Inouye (which is now written Inoue) and Uyeda (which is now written Ueda). Japanese money has the following denominations:

Coins

1 yen	**ichi-en dama**
5 yen	**go-en dama**
10 yen	**jū-en dama**
50 yen	**go-jū-en dama**
100 yen	**hayku-en dama**
500 yen	**go-hyaku-en dama**

Notes

1,000 yen	**sen-en satsu**
5,000 yen	**go-sen-en satsu**
10,000 yen	**ichi-man-en satsu**

FOREIGN CURRENCY

The Japanese names of some major foreign currencies are:

doru	dollar
maruku	mark
pondo	pound

ADDITIONAL VOCABULARY

bāgen	bargain, sale
bunbōguya	stationery store
chūmon suru (shimasu)	to order
depāto	department store

garō	art gallery
gasorin sutando	gas station
ginkō	bank
hanaya	florist
hangaku	half-price
honya	bookstore
hyakkaten	department store
kaimono o suru shimasu	to shop
kanamonoya	hardware store
konbiniensu sutoa	convenience store
kottōhinya	antique shop
kurīninguya	dry cleaners
kusuriya	drugstore
menzeihinten	duty-free shop
mise	shop
nikuya	butcher shop
(o)kashiya	confectionery
(o)kyaku-sama	customer
omochaya	toy store
otsuri	change
pan'ya	bakery
resutoran	restaurant
sakanaya	fish store
sakaya	liquor store
shashinya	photo shop
shōten	shop
shōten-gai	shopping arcade
sūpā	supermarket
yaoya	greengrocers
yakkyoku	pharmacy
yūbinkyoku	post office
zaiko	inventory on hand

ANSWERS TO EXERCISES

1. a. *bāgen* b. *garō* c. *konbiniensu sutoa* d. *sūpā* (shortened)
2. a. *Jū guramu kudasai.* b. *Kyū-jū guramu kudasai.*
   c. *Ni-hyaku guramu kudasai.* d. *Ni-hyaku-go-jū guramu kudasai.*
3. a. *Hitotsu kudasai.* b. *Mittsu kudasai.* c. *Itsutsu kudasai.*
   d. *Nanatsu kudasai.*
4. a. *Kore o misete kudasai.* b. *Sore o misete kudasai.*
   c. *Are o misete kudasai.*
5. a. *Akai no o misete kudasai.* b. *Aoi no o misete kudasai.*
   c. *Chīsai no o misete kudasai.* d. *Motto chīsai no o misete kudasai.* e. *Ōkii no o misete kudasai.* f. *Motto ōkii no o misete kudasai.*

CAN YOU GET BY?

TEST

Try these exercises when you have finished the course. The answers are on pages 91 and 92.

1. You've just arrived at Narita Airport. The customs' officer points to a package and asks, *Kore wa nan desu ka?* Tell him it's whiskey.
2. You're at the information desk. Ask the person working there to recommend a good hotel.
3. You don't know what something is, or what it's called. How do you ask "What is this?"
4. Introduce yourself to someone else.
5. What do you say when you enter someone's house?
6. Do you know the following adjectives? Good, attractive, big, small, hot, cold, expensive.
7. When someone tells you your Japanese is terrific, what do you say?
8. You need to leave a meeting or gathering. What do you say?
9. Ask where a taxi stand is.

10. Buy a round-trip ticket to Kyoto for yourself and your partner.
11. You're in a taxi. Tell the driver to take you to the train station.
12. Ask directions to the post office.
13. You sit down in a coffee shop. Can you order a cup of coffee?
14. Suggest to a friend that you have dinner together.
15. At the restaurant you're given two choices. How do you say you prefer beer?
16. Ask to see if the restaurant serves tempura.
17. At a business meeting, you introduce your boss, the company president.
18. Give "just a little something" to your Japanese business partner.
19. Thank your business partner for all he or she has done for you.
20. Tell your business partner you'd like continued good relations in the future.
21. As you leave your appointment, tell your business partner you're looking forward to meeting again.
22. At a store, you ask for 10 grams of that one.
23. Ask a vendor for three items.
24. Ask a salesperson to show you something on the shelf over there.
25. Ask to be shown a bigger one.

ANSWERS

1. *Uisukī desu.* 2. *Ii hoteru o shōkai shite kudasai.* 3. *Kore wa nan desu ka?* 4. *Hajimemashite. . . . desu.* 5. *Ojama itashimasu.* 6. *Ii, kirei, ōkii, chīsai, atsui, samui, takai.* 7. *Iie, jōzu de wa arimasen.* 8. *Sorosoro, shitsurei shimasu.* 9. *Takushī noriba wa doko desu ka?* 10. *Kyoto, ōfuku, ni-mai kudasai.* 11. *Eki made,*

itte kudasai. 12. *Yūbin kyoku wa, dō ikeba ii n'desu ka?*
13. *Kōhī o kudasai.* 14. *Shokuji o shimashō ka?* 15. *Bīru no hō ga ii n'desu.* 16. *Tenpura ga arimasu ka?* 17. *Kochira wa uchi no shachō desu.* 18. *Tsumaranai mono desu ga, dōzo.* 19. *Iro iro, osewa ni narimashita.* 20. *Kore kara mo, yoroshiku onegai shimasu.* 21. *Mata, chikai uchi ni aimashō.* 22. *Sore o, jū guramu kudasai.* 23. *Mittsu kudasai.* 24. *Are o misete kudasai.* 25. *Motto ōkii no o misete kudasai.*

REFERENCE SECTION

THE JAPANESE SYLLABARY

RŌMAJI AND HIRAGANA

a あ	i い	u う	e え	o お
ka か	ki き	ku く	ke け	ko こ
sa さ	shi し	su す	se せ	so そ
ta た	chi ち	tsu つ	te て	to と
na な	ni に	nu ぬ	ne ね	no の
ha は	hi ひ	fu ふ	he へ	ho ほ
ma ま	mi み	mu む	me め	mo も
ya や		yu ゆ		yo よ
ra ら	ri り	ru る	re れ	ro ろ
wa わ				wo を
n ん				

ga が	gi ぎ	gu ぐ	ge げ	go ご
za ざ	ji じ	zu ず	ze ぜ	zo ぞ
da だ	ji ぢ	zu づ	de で	do ど
ba ば	bi び	bu ぶ	be べ	bo ぼ
pa ぱ	pi ぴ	pu ぷ	pe ぺ	po ぽ

kya きゃ	kyu きゅ	kyo きょ
sha しゃ	shu しゅ	sho しょ
cha ちゃ	chu ちゅ	cho ちょ
nya にゃ	nyu にゅ	nyo にょ
hya ひゃ	hyu ひゅ	hyo ひょ
mya みゃ	myu みゅ	myo みょ
rya りゃ	ryu りゅ	ryo りょ
gya ぎゃ	gyu ぎゅ	gyo ぎょ

ja (zya) じゃ	ju(zyu) じゅ	jo(zyo) じょ
ja (dya) ぢゃ	ju(dyu) ぢゅ	jo(dyo) ぢょ
bya びゃ	byu びゅ	byo びょ
pya ぴゃ	pyu ぴゅ	pyo ぴょ

RŌMAJI AND KATAKANA

a	ア	i	イ	u	ウ	e	エ	o	オ
ka	カ	ki	キ	ku	ク	ke	ケ	ko	コ
sa	サ	shi	シ	su	ス	se	セ	so	ソ
ta	タ	chi	チ	tsu	ツ	te	テ	to	ト
na	ナ	ni	ニ	nu	ヌ	ne	ネ	no	ノ
ha	ハ	hi	ヒ	fu	フ	he	ヘ	ho	ホ
ma	マ	mi	ミ	mu	ム	me	メ	mo	モ
ya	ヤ			yu	ユ			yo	ヨ
ra	ラ	ri	リ	ru	ル	re	レ	ro	ロ
wa	ワ							wo	ヲ
n	ン								

ga	ガ	gi	ギ	gu	グ	ge	ゲ	go	ゴ
za	ザ	ji	ジ	zu	ズ	ze	ゼ	zo	ゾ
da	ダ	ji	ヂ	zu	ヅ	de	デ	do	ド
ba	バ	bi	ビ	bu	ブ	be	ベ	bo	ボ
pa	パ	pi	ピ	pu	プ	pe	ペ	po	ポ

kya	キャ	kyu	キュ	kyo	キョ
sha	シャ	shu	シュ	sho	ショ
cha	チャ	chu	チュ	cho	チョ
nya	ニャ	nyu	ニュ	nyo	ニョ

hya ヒャ	hyu ヒュ	hyo ヒョ
mya ミャ	myu ミュ	myo ミョ
rya リャ	ryu リュ	ryo リョ
gya ギャ	gyu ギュ	gyo ギョ
ja (zya) ジャ	ju(zyu) ジュ	jo(zyo) ジョ
ja (dya) ヂャ	ju(dyu) ヂュ	jo(dyo) ヂョ
bya ビャ	byu ビュ	byo ビョ
pya ピャ	pyu ピュ	pyo ピョ

NUMBERS

CARDINAL NUMBERS

There are two ways to count. The Japanese style of counting goes up to ten. Use these numbers when you do not need to use a counter (sheet, head, order, etc.). In other words, use them when you don't need to be specific. You'd say, *Hitotsu kudasai*. (I'd like one, please) rather than *Ichi-mai kudasai*. (I'd like one sheet, please.)

1	*hitotsu*	6	*muttsu*
2	*futatsu*	7	*nanatsu*
3	*mittsu*	8	*yattsu*
4	*yottsu*	9	*kokonotsu*
5	*itsutsu*	10	*tō*

The Chinese style of counting is as follows:

1	*ichi*
2	*ni*
3	*san*
4	*yon, shi*
5	*go*
6	*roku*
7	*nana, shichi*
8	*hachi*
9	*kyū, ku*
10	*jū*
11	*jū-ichi*
12	*jū-ni*
13	*jū-san*
14	*jū-shi (jūyon)*
15	*jū-go*
16	*jū-roku*
17	*jū-shichi (jū-nana)*
18	*jū-hachi*
19	*jū-ku (jū-kyū)*
20	*ni-jū*
30	*san-jū*
40	*yon-jū*
50	*go-jū*
60	*roku-jū*
70	*nana-jū (shichi-jū)*
80	*hachi-jū*
90	*kyū-jū*
100	*hyaku*
110, 120 . . .	*hyaku-jū, hyaku-ni-jū . . . .*
200	*ni-hyaku*
300	*san-byaku*
400	*yon-hyaku*
500	*go-hyaku*

600	*rop-pyaku*
700	*nana-hyaku*
800	*hap-pyaku*
900	*kyū-hyaku*
1,000	*sen*
1,100; 1,200 . . .	*sen-hyaku; sen-ni-hyaku . . .*
2,000	*ni-sen*
10,000	*ichi-man*
11,000; 12,000 . . .	*ichi-man-is-sen; ichi-man-ni-sen . . .*
20,000	*ni-man*
1,000,000	*hyaku-man*
1,100,000	*hyaku-jū-man*
1,200,000 . . .	*hyaku-ni-jū-man*
3,000,000	*san-byaku-man*

TIME OF DAY

A.M.	*gozen*	hours	*ji*
P.M.	*gogo*	minutes	*fun*
noon	*hiru*		

1 o'clock	*ichi-ji*	7 o'clock	*shichi-ji*
2 o'clock	*ni-ji*	8 o'clock	*hachi-ji*
3 o'clock	*san-ji*	9 o'clock	*ku-ji*
4 o'clock	*yo-ji*	10 o'clock	*jū-ji*
5 o'clock	*go-ji*	11 o'clock	*jū-ichi-ji*
6 o'clock	*roku-ji*	12 o'clock	*jū-ni-ji*

1:15	*ichi-ji jū-go-fun*
1:30	*ichi-ji han*
1:45	*ichi-ji yon-jū go-fun*

DAYS OF THE WEEK

Monday	*Getsuyōbi*	Friday	*Kinyōbi*
Tuesday	*Kayōbi*	Saturday	*Doyōbi*
Wednesday	*Suiyōbi*	Sunday	*Nichiyōbi*
Thursday	*Mokuyōbi*		

DAYS OF THE MONTH

1st	*tsuitachi*	6th	*muika*
2nd	*futsuka*	7th	*nanoka*
3rd	*mikka*	8th	*yōka*
4th	*yokka*	9th	*kokonoka*
5th	*itsuka*	10th	*tōka*

11th, 12th, 13th	*jū-ichi-nichi, jū-ni-nichi, jū-san-nichi*, etc. (except for the 14th)
14th	*jū-yokka*
20th	*tsuitachi*
21st, 22nd	*ni-jū-ichi-nichi, ni-jū-ni-nichi*, etc. (except for the 24th)
24th	*ni-jū-yokka*
30th	*san-jū-nichi*
last day	*misoka*

MONTHS OF THE YEAR

January	*Ichi-gatsu*	July	*Shichi-gatsu*
February	*Ni-gatsu*	August	*Hachi-gatsu*
March	*San-gatsu*	September	*Ku-gatsu*
April	*Shi-gatsu*	October	*Jū-gatsu*
May	*Go-gatsu*	November	*Jū-ichi-gatsu*
June	*Roku-gatsu*	December	*Jū-ni-gatsu*

LENGTHS OF TIME

one day	*ichi-nichi*
two days	*futsuka-kan*
three days	*mikka-kan*
four day	*yokka-kan*
five days	*itsuka-kan*
six days	*muika-kan*

one week, two weeks . . .	*is-shū-kan, ni-shū-kan* . . .
one month, two months . . .	*ik-ka-getsu (hitotsuki), ni-ka-getsu* . . .
one year, two years . . .	*ichi-nen-kan, ni-nen-kan* . . .

WORD LISTS

> How do you say, "Good bye?"

> Sayōnara. That's too easy, Babs.

JAPANESE—ENGLISH

A

achira (formal form of *asoko*)
aisatsu courtesy call, greeting
akai red (adj.)
akaji debt, deficit, in the red
amai sweet (adj.)
amari [not] very (when used with *de wa arimasen* or other negative verbs and adjectives)
Amerika America, United States
Amerikajin an American
ane one's own older sister (compare **onēsan**)
ani one's own elder brother (compare **onīsan***)
annaijo information booth
aoi green, blue (adj.)
are that one
Are o misete kudasai. Show me that one, please.
Arigatō gozaimasu. Thank you. (humble, polite form of *arigatai n'desu*)
aru (arimasu) to exist, to be
aruku (arukimasu) to walk
asa (go)han, chōshoku breakfast
ashita tomorrow
asoko over there

atchi over there (informal form of *asoko*)
atsui hot (adj.)
awabi abalone

B

bāgen bargain, sale
baiten kiosk
basu bus
basu tei bus stop
beddo bed
bijinesu hoteru business hotel
bīru beer
boeki masatsu trade dispute
buchō director
bunbōguya stationery store

C

chichi one's own father (compare **otōsan***)
chikai close, nearby (adj.)
chikai uchi ni before too long
chikatetsu subway
chikatetsu no eki subway station
chīsai small
chizu map
chōdo exactly

chōdo ii   just right
chōshoku, asa (go)han   breakfast
chotto   a little bit
chotto chīsai   a little small
Chūka ryōri   Chinese cuisine
chūmon suru (shimasu)   to order
chūsoku, hiru (go)han   lunch

D

daisuki   a favorite [of mine]
danbō   heating
de   by (particle: indicates the means by which something is done)
de wa   well then
deguchi   exit
demo   but
denwa   telephone
depāto, hyakatten   department store
deshō   isn't it (a speculative form of *desu*)
desu   is (polite form of *da*)
desu kara   because
dō   how (less formal than *ikaga*)
dō ikeba   how should I go (conditional form of *iku*)
Dō itashimashite.   Think nothing of it.
dochira   where (polite form of *doko*)
doko   where
donburi   cooked rice topped with various vegetables and meat
dono gurai   how long, how much
dorai-kurīningu   dry cleaning
doru   dollar
dotchi   where (informal form of *doko*)
dōzo   please [come in, accept it]

E

e   to (particle: indicates movement toward some point)
ebi   shrimp

eiga   movie
eki   train station
emu-saizu   medium size
en   yen
erebētā   elevator
eru-saizu   large size

F

fuku-shachō   executive vice-president
funabin   surface mail
futari   two persons
futatsu   two [items]
futatsu-me   second (ordinal no.)
futon   Japanese-style bed
futsū, kakueki teisha   regular train (stops at all stations)

G

ga   but
. . . ga suki desu   I like . . .
gakusei   student
garō   art gallery
gasorin sutando   gas station
genkan   portico
genzaichi   where you are now
gijutsu   technology
ginkō   bank
gogo   P.M.
(Go)chisō-sama deshita.   Thanks for a delicious meal.
(go)han   cooked rice, a meal
(go)shōkai shimasu   to introduce (polite, honorific form of *shōkai suru*)
gozen   A.M.
guramu   gram
gurīnsha   first class (green car)
gyūnyū   milk

H

haha   one's own mother (compare *okāsan*)
hai   yes, all right, I see

Hajimemashite. How do you do?
hanaya florist
hangaku half-price
hayai early (adj.)
heya-dai cost of a room
hidari ni magaru turn left
hijōguchi emergency exit
hikui low (adj.)
hinshitsu quality
hiru (go)han, chūsoku lunch
hisho secretary
hitori one person
hitotsu one
hodōkyō pedestrian overpass
hontō ni truly
honya bookstore
hoteru hotel
hotto miruku hot milk
hyakkaten, depāto department
 store

I

ichi-mai one ticket
ii good (adj.)
ika squid
ikaga how
iku (ikimasu) to go
ikura salmon roe
Ikura desu ka? How much is it?
imōto younger sister
ippaku one night's stay
Irasshaimase. Come in, welcome.
 (Honorific, imperative form of
 kuru)
iro iro various, in many ways
iru (irimasu) to need
isogu (isogimasu) to hurry
Isoide kudasai. Please hurry.

J

jā well then (contraction for *de wa*)
jā, mata well, [see you] again
jichō senior manager
jiko shōkai self introduction
jōmu managing director

jōshaken regular railway ticket
 (cost determined by the mileage)
jōzu good at, skillful
jūsu orange soda

K

ka (particle: indicates a question)
ka nē [I] wonder (particles: *ka*
 indicates a question, *nē* seeks
 affirmation)
kabu stock
kabushiki gaisha corporation
kachō manager
kado street corner
kaeru (kaerimasu) to return
kagi key
kaichō chairman
kaidan stairs
kaigi meeting
kaimono o suru (shimasu) to
 shop
kaisoku densha rapid-service train
 (stops infrequently)
kakarichō, shunin supervisor
kaku kakueki (kakimasu) to write
kakueki teisha, futsū regular train
 (stops at all stations)
kanai one's wife
kanamonoya hardware store
karai salty, spicy (adj.)
karaoke singing to a taped musical
 accompaniment (lit. empty
 orchestra)
karē raisu curry rice
karui light weight (adj.)
kashi Fahrenheit
kashikomarimashita [I]
 understand (polite, completed
 form of *kashikomaru*)
kata person (honorific)
katamichi one way
kau (kaimasu) to buy
kawase rēto exchange rate
kazoku family
keiei management

keiki cake

keiyakusho contract

kenbaiki automated ticket machines

ki o tsukatte itadaite you're being so considerate

kiiroi yellow (adj.)

kin'en seki non-smoking seat

kippu ticket

kirei nice, pretty

kiro, kiroguramu kilogram

kiro, kirōmetoru kilometer

kiru (kimasu) to wear

kissaten coffee shop

kitsui tight, arduous (adj.)

kitsune udon noodles with fried tōfu

kōban police box

kōcha black tea

kochira here, this person [here] (polite form of *koko*)

kodomo child

kōhī coffee

koin rokkā coin locker

kōjō factory

koko here

kokoa hot chocolate

kōkūbin airmail

Kōkūbin de onegai shimasu. By airmail, please.

Konban wa. Good evening.

konbiniensu sutoa convenience store

konki this fiscal year

kono this

kono jūsho this address

kōra cola

kore this one

kore kara mo from now on (as before)

Kore o kudasai. Please, give me this one.

Kore wa nan desu ka? What is this?

kōsaten intersection

kōshō negotiations

kosuto cost

kotchi here (informal form of *koko*)

koto an (abstract) thing

kottōhinya antique shop

kudasai please

kurīninguya dry cleaners

kuroi black (adj.)

kuroji surplus, profit, in the black

kusuriya drugstore

kutsu shoes

kutsu bera shoehorn

Kuzushite kudasaimasu ka? Could you break [this bill], please?

kyanseru, torikeshi cancel

kyapuseru hoteru capsule hotel

kyō today

kyōdai siblings

Kyōshuku desu. [I'm] truly grateful.

kyūkō express train

M

made until, up to (particle: indicates distance, duration, inclusion)

magatta to turn (completed form of *magaru*)

maguro tuna

-mai counter for sheetlike objects

makura pillow

mantan full tank [of gas]

Mantan ni shite kudasai. Fill it up with gas, please.

maruku [German] mark

massugu straight ahead

matsu (machimasu) to wait

meishi name card

menzeihinten duty-free shop

mētoru meter

michi road

michi, dōri street

midori no madoguchi window for express tickets

migi right

migi ni magaru turn right

mijikai short (adj.)

miru (mimasu) to see
miruku milk
mise, shōten shop
misoshiru miso soup
mitsumori estimate
mizu water
mizutaki chicken simmered in broth (usually cooked at your table)
mizuwari whiskey and water
mo also (particle: used to include something or someone)
mō already
mōfu blanket
mono a (tangible) thing
mōsu (mōshimasu) to call
motto more
motto ōkii bigger
motto yasui more inexpensive
musuko son
musume daughter
muzukashii difficult

N

nagai tsukiai long-standing relationship
nagai long (adj.)
nama-bīru draft beer
nan, nani what
Nani ga arimasu ka? What do you have?
nani mo nai nothing much
n'desu contraction for *no desu*
nē (particle: emphasis, for seeking affirmation)
ni to, toward (particle: showing destination, place or time)
ni at (particle: showing location)
nigai bitter (adj.)
nigirizushi bite-sized bits of cooked, vinegared rice topped with fresh seafood
Nihon Japan
Nihon ryōri Japanese cuisine

Nihongo the Japanese language
Nihonjin a Japanese person
nikuya butcher shop
nimotsu azukarijo luggage check-in
no (particle: shows possession)
. . . no hō ga ii . . . is better.
nomi no ichi flea market
nomimono a drink
nomu (nomimasu) to drink
norimaki cooked rice with vegetables wrapped in seaweed (*nori*)
nyōbō wife

O

o (particle: indicates verb object)
oagari kudasai come in (honorific, imperative form of *agaru*)
(o)aiso the bill at a sushi shop
obasan aunt
obāsan grandmother
(o)cha Japanese (green) tea
ōdan hodō pedestrian crossing
ōfuku round trip
(O)genki desu ka? How are you?
Ogorimashō. My treat.
(O)hayō gozaimasu. Good morning. (polite, humble form of *hayai*)
(o)hiya cold drinking water
oishii delicious, tasty
(O)jama itashimasu. Forgive the intrusion (humble, polite form of *jama suru*)
ojisan uncle
ojīsan grandfather
(O)kagesama de. Thanks to you.
(o)kane money
(o)kanjō the bill
okāsan someone else's mother
okashiya confectionery
ōkii big (adj.)
(o)kyaku-sama customer

(o)manjū Japanese cakes
omochaya toy store
omoi heavy (adj.)
omou (omoimasu) to think
onēsan someone else's older sister
(o)nimotsu luggage
(o)nimotsu azukarijo luggage check in
onīsan someone else's older brother
orenji jūsu orange juice
(o)sake rice wine
(O)sewa ni narimashita. I'm indebted to your kindness.
otearai, toire toilet
otona adult
otōsan someone else's father
otōto younger brother
(o)tsuri change
oyako chicken and eggs (literally, parents and children)
oyako donburi rice topped with chicken and eggs

P

pan'ya bakery
pasupōto passport
patento, tokkyo patent
pondo pound

R

raiki next fiscal year
rāmen Chinese-style noodles
remon tī black tea with lemon
resutoran restaurant
rittoru liter
rūmu sābisu room service
ryokan Japanese-style inn
ryōkin fare
ryūtsū distribution

S

sābisu ryō service charge
sakana fish
sakanaya fishstore
sakaya liquor store
samui cold [weather] (adj.)
sashimi raw fish
sayōnara goodbye
seisanjo fare adjustment window
semai crowded (adj.)
senchi, senchimētoru centimeter
senmu senior managing director
sentaku laundry
sesshi Centigrade
setsubi tōshi capital spending
settai suru (shimasu) to entertain
shabushabu beef simmered in broth
shachō chief executive officer, president
shakkin loan
shashin-shū photography collection
shashinya photo shop
shichiya second-hand shop
shihon capital
shingō traffic light
shinu (shinimasu) to die
shiroi white (adj.)
shitei seki reserved seat
Shitsurei suru (shimasu). It's time for me to leave.
shiyakusho city hall
shōkai suru (shimasu) to introduce
shokuji a meal
shōshō a little while
Shōshō omachi kudasai. Please wait a moment.
shōtai suru to invite
shōten, mise shop
shōten-gai shopping arcade
shujin husband
shunin, kakarichō supervisor

Sō shimashō. Let's do that.

Sō de mo arimasen. Not necessarily.

Sō desu ka? Is that right?

soba buckwheat noodles

sochira there (polite form of *soko*)

sōda soda

soko there

sore that one

Sore ni suru (shimasu). I'll take that.

Sore o kudasai. Please give me that one.

sorosoro it's about time, by and by

sotchi there (informal form of *soho*)

Sumimasen. Excuse me. Sorry.

sūpā supermarket

supagettī spaghetti

surippa slippers

suru (shimasu) to do

sushi vinegared rice with fresh sea food and vegetables

sushiya a sushi shop

T

tabemono food

taberu (tabemasu) to eat (polite form)

Taishikan embassy

taizai suru (shimasu) to stay

takai tall, expensive (adj.)

tako octopus

takushī taxi

takushī noriba taxi stand

tatami rice-straw mat

teishoku a fixed menu

tenpura tempura (deep-fried vegetables, seafood, etc.)

tenpura udon noodles with tempura

terebi television

to (particle to indicate what is thought, felt, said)

to and (particle: used to list things)

toire, otearai toilet

tokkyūken express ticket

tokoro place

tomaru (tomarimasu) to stop

tomodachi, yūjin friend

tonkatsu pork cutlet

tori street

torihiki business, transactions, dealings

torikeshi, kyanseru cancel

toro the fatty belly flesh of a tuna

tōshi investment

Tsumaranai mono desu ga, dōzo . . . This is nothing much, but please . . .

tsumetai cold [liquid]

U

uchi house

uchi no our

udon thick white noodles

uisukī whiskey

uketsuke reception

unagi broiled marinated eels

uni sea urchin

unsō shipping

uriba selling place

W

wa as for (particle: indicates a topic)

wain wine

warikan everyone's pays for his or her own share of the bill

washitsu Japanese-style room

washoku Japanese cuisine

watakushi I

wazuka it's nothing much

Y

yakitori charcoal-grilled chicken, chicken liver, and green unions on a bamboo stick

yakkyoku   pharmacy
yaoya   greengrocers
yappari   as expected
yasui   cheap (adj.)
yobu (yobimasu)   to call
Yoku irasshaimashita.   Thanks for coming.
Yoroshiku onegai shimasu.
   Pleased to make your acquaintance.
yōshitsu   Western–style room
yōshoku   Western cuisine
yūbinkyoku   post office

yūjin, tomodachi   friend
yurui   loose (adj.)
yūshoku, yūgohan   dinner

Z

zabuton   a cushion
zaiko   inventory, stock
zehi   by all means
zeikin   tax
zenki   last fiscal year, previous period

ENGLISH—JAPANESE

A

A.M.   gozen
abalone   awabi
adult   otona
airmail   kōkūbin
all right; yes, I see   hai
already   mō
also   mo (particle: used to include something)
America, United States   Amerika
and   to (particle: used to list things)
antique shop   kottōhinya
art gallery   garō
as for   wa (particle: indicates a topic)
as expected   yappari
at   ni (particle: showing location)
aunt   obasan
automated ticket machines   kenbaiki

B

bakery   pan'ya
bank   ginkō
bargain, **sale**   bāgen
to be, to exist   aru (arimasu)
because   desu kara
bed   beddo
beef simmered in broth   shabu shabu
beer   bīru
before too long   chikai uchi ni
big   ōkii (adj.)
bigger   motto ōkii
bill   (o)kanjō, (o)aiso (at a sushi shop)
bite-sized bits of cooked rice and seafood   nigirizushi
bitter   nigai (adj.)
black   kuroi (adj.)
black tea   kōcha
blanket   mōfu

blue, green   aoi (adj.)
bookstore   honya
breakfast   choshoku, asa (go)han
buckwheat noodles   soba
bus stop   basu tei
business hotel   bijinesu hoteru
business transaction, **dealings**   torihiki
but   ga
but, however   demo
butcher shop   nikuya
to buy   kau (kaimasu)
by   de (particle: means by which)
by all means   zehi
By airmail, please.   Kōkūbin de onegai shimasu.

C

cake   keiki
to call, **to say**   mōsu (mōshimasu)
to call out   yobu (yobimasu)
cancel   kyanseru, torikeshi
capital   shihon
capital spending   setsubi tōshi
capsule hotel   kapuseru hoteru
Centigrade   sesshi
centimeter   senchi, senchimētoru
chairman   kaichō
change   (o)tsuri
charcoal-grilled chicken   yakitori
cheap   yasui (adj.)
chicken and eggs on rice   oya-ko donburi
chicken simmered in broth   mizutaki
chief executive officer, president   shachō
child   kodomo
Chinese cuisine   chūka ryōri
Chinese-style noodles   rāmen
city hall   shiyakusho
close, nearby   chikai (adj.)

coffee shop kissaten
coin locker koin rokkā
cola kōra
cold [liquid] tsumetai (adj.)
cold drinking water (o)hiya
Come in, welcome. Irasshaimase.
come in oagari kudasai
confectionery okashiya
contract keiyakusho
convenience store konbiniensu
    sutoa
cooked rice, a meal (go)han
**cooked rice topped with
    vegetables and meats** donburi
corporation kabushiki gaisha
cost kosuto
cost of a room heya-dai
Could you break this bill, please?
    Kuzushite kudasaimasu ka?
counter for sheetlike objects
    -mai
crowded semai (adj.)
curry rice karē raisu
cushion zabuton
customer (o)kyaku-sama

D

daughter musume
debt, deficit, in the red akaji
delicious oishii
department store depāto,
    hyakkaten
to die shinu (shinimasu)
difficult muzukashii
dinner yūshoku, yū (go)han
director buchō
distribution ryūtsū
to do suru (shimasu)
dollar doru
draft beer nama-bīru
to drink nomu (nomimasu)
drug store kusuriya
dry clean dorai-kurīningu
dry cleaners dorai-kurīninguya
duty-free shop menzei hinten

E

early hayai (adj.)
to eat taberu (tabemasu)
eel unagi
elder brother ani, onīsan (if some-
    one else's)
elevator erebētā
embassy taishikan
emergency exit hijōguchi
to entertain settai suru (shimasu)
estimate mitsumori
exactly chōdo
exchange rate kawase rēto
Excuse me. Sumimasen.
executive vice-president fuku-
    shachō
to exist, to be aru (arimasu)
exit deguchi
expensive, tall takai
express ticket tokkyūken

F

factory kōjō
Fahrenheit kashi
family kazoku
fare ryōkin
fare adjustment window seisanjo
father chichi, otōsan (if someone
    else's)
Fill it up with gas, please.
    Mantan ni shite kudasai.
first class (green car) gurīnsha
fish sakana
fishstore sakanaya
fixed menu teishoku
flea market nomi no ichi
florist hanaya
food tabemono
Forgive the intrusion. (O)jama
    itashimasu.
friend tomodachi, yūjin
from now on (as before) kore
    kara mo
full tank [of gas] mantan

G

gas station gasorin sutando
to go iku (ikimasu)
good ii (adj.)
good at, skillful jōzu
Goodbye. Sayōnara. Jā, mata.
Good evening. Konban wa.
Good morning. Ohayō gozaimasu.
gram guramu, kiroguramu
grandfather ojīsan
grandmother obāsan
green, blue aoi (adj.)
greengrocers yaoya

H

half-price hangaku
hardware store kanamonoya
heating danbō
heavy omoi (adj.)
here koko, kotchi (informal), kochi-ra (formal)
hot chocolate kokoa
hot milk hotto miruku
hotel hoteru
house uchi
how dō
How are you? (O)genki desu ka?
How do you do? Hajimemashite.
how long, how much dono gurai
How much is it? Ikura desu ka?
How should I go? Dō ikeba ii n'desu ka?
however, but demo
to hurry isogu (isogimasu)
husband shujin

I

I watakushi
I like . . . . . . ga suki desu.
I understand kashikomarimashita (polite form of *kashikomaru*)
I wonder ka nē (particles: *ka* indicates a question, *nē* seeks affirmation)

I'll pay the bill. Ogotte agemashō.
I'll take that. Sore ni shimasu.
I'm indebted to your kindness. (O)sewa ni narimashita.
information booth annaijo
intersection kōsaten
to introduce shōkai suru (shimasu)
inventory, stock zaiko
investment tōshi
to invite shōtai suru (shimasu)
is desu
. . . is better . . . no hō ga ii

Is that right? Sō desu ka?
isn't it, it is deshō
It's nothing much. Wazuka desu.
It's about time to leave, by and by sorosoro
It's time for me to leave. Shitsurei shimasu.

J

Japan Nihon
Japanese cakes (o)manjū
Japanese cuisine Nihon ryōri
Japanese (green) tea (o)cha
Japanese language Nihongo
Japanese person Nihonjin
Japanese-style inn ryokan
Japanese-style room washitsu
just right chōdo ii

K

key kagi
kilogram kiro, kiroguramu
kilometer kiro, kiromētoru
kiosk baiten

L

large [size] eru-saizu
laundry sentaku
Let's do that. Sō shimashō.

light karui (adj.)
liquor store sakaya
liter rittoru
loan shakkin
long nagai (adj.)
long-standing relationship nagai tsukiai
loose yurui (adj.)
low hikui (adj.)
luggage (o)nimotsu
luggage check in nimotsu azukarijo
lunch chūshoku, hiru (go)han

M

management keiei
manager kachō
managing director jōmu
map chizu
mark (German currency) maruku
meal, dinner shokuji
medium size emu-saizu
meeting kaigi
meter mētoru
milk miruku
miso soup miso shiru
money (o)kane
more motto
more inexpensive motto yasui
mother haha, okāsan (if someone else's)
movie eiga
My treat. Ogorimashō.

N

name card meishi
to need iru (irimasu)
negotiations kōshō
next fiscal year raiki
nice, pretty kirei
non-smoking seat kin'en seki
noodles soba (buckwheat), udon (wheat), rāmen (Chinese)

noodles with tempura tenpura udon
Not necessarily. Sō de mo arimasen.
nothing much nani mo nai
Nothing much, but please . . . Tsumaranai mono desu ga . . .

O

octopus tako
older sister ane, onēsan (if someone else's)
one night's stay ippaku
one person hitori
one ticket ichi-mai
one way katamichi
orange juice orenji jūsu
to order chūmon suru (shimasu)
our uchi no
over there asoko, atchi (informal), achira (formal)

P

P.M. gogo
passport passupōto
patent patento, tokkyo
pedestrian crossing odon hodō
pedestrian overpass hodōkyō
person kata (honorific)
pharmacy yakkyoku
photo shop shashinya
photography collection shashin-shū
pillow makura
place tokoro
please kudasai
please [come in] dōzo
Please give me that one. Sore o kudasai.
Please give me this one. Kore o kudasai.
Please hurry. Isoide kudasai.
Please wait a moment. Shōshō omachi kudasai.

Pleased to make your acquaintance. Yoroshiku onegai shimasu.
police box kōban
pork cutlet tonkatsu
portico genkan
post office yūbinkyoku
pound (English currency) pondo
pretty, nice kirei
previous period zenki

Q

quality hinshitsu

R

rapid-service train kaisoku densha
raw fish sashimi
reception uketsuke
red akai (adj.)
regular railway ticket jōshaken
regular train futsū, kakueki teisha
reserved seat shitei seki
restaurant resutoran
to return kaeru (kaerimasu)
rice wine (o)sake
rice-straw mat tatami
right migi
road michi
room service rūmu sābisu
round trip ōfuku

S

sale, bargain bāgen
salmon roe ikura
salty, spicy karai (adj.)
to say, to call mōsu (mōshimasu)
sea urchin uni
second futatsu-me (ordinal no.)
second-hand shop shichiya
secretary hisho
to see miru (mimasu)
self-introduction jiko shōkai
senior managing director senmu

senior manager jichō
service charge sābisu ryō
shipping unsō
shoehorn kutsu bera
shoes kutsu
to shop kaimono o suru (shimasu)
shop mise, shōten
shopping arcade shōtengai
short mijikai (adj.)
Show me that one, please. Are o misete kudasai.
shrimp ebi
siblings kyōdai
singing to taped accompaniment karaoke
skillful, good at jōzu
slippers surippa
small chīsai
soda sōda
son musuko
Sorry. Sumimasen.
spaghetti supagettī
squid ika
stairs kaidan
stationery store bunbōguya
to stay overnight taizai suru (shimasu)
stock kabu
to stop tomaru (tomarimasu)
straight ahead massugu
street tōri
street corner kado
student gakusei
subway chikatetsu
supermarket sūpā
supervisor shunin, kakarichō
surface mail funabin
surplus, profit, in the black kuroji
sweet amai (adj.)

T

tall, expensive takai
tax zeikin
taxi takushī
taxi stand takushī noriba

technology gijutsu
telephone denwa
television terebi
tempura tenpura
Thank you. Arigatō gozaimasu.
Thanks for a delicious meal.
  (Go)chisō-sama deshita.
Thanks for coming. Yoku
  irasshaimashita.
Thanks to you. (O)kagesama de.
that one sore
that one (over there) are
there soko, sotchi (informal), sochira (formal)
thing (abstract) koto
thing (concrete) mono
to think omou (omoimasu)
Think nothing of it. Dō
  itashimashite.
this kono
this fiscal year konki
this one kore
this person [here] kochira
ticket kippu
tight kitsui (adj.)
to e (particle: movement toward
  some point)
to, toward ni (particle: showing
  direction)
today kyō
toilet (o)tearai, toire
tomorrow ashita
toy store omochaya
trade dispute bōeki masatsu
traffic light shingō
train station eki
truly hontō ni
tuna maguro, toro (the belly flesh of
  a tuna)
to turn magaru (magarimasu)
to turn right migi ni magaru
  (magarimasu)
to turn left hidari ni magaru
  (magarimasu)
two [items] futatsu
two persons futari

U

uncle ojisan
to understand kashikomaru
  (kashikomarimasu)
until, up to made (particle:
  indicates distance)

V

various, in many ways iro iro
vinegared rice sushi

W

to wait matsu (machimasu)
to walk aruku (arukimasu)
water mizu
to wear kiru (kimasu)
well then de wa, jā (contracted
  form)
Western cuisine yōshoku
Western-style room yōshitsu
what nani, nan
What do you have? Nani ga
  arimasu ka?
What is this? Kore wa nan desu ka?
where doko, dotchi (informal),
  dochira (formal)
where you are now genzaichi
whiskey uisukī
whiskey and water mizuwari
white shiroi (adj.)
wife kanai (one's wife), okusan
  (someone's wife)
window for express tickets
  midori no madoguchi
wine wain
to write kaku (kakimasu)

Y

yellow kiiroi (adj.)
yen en
yes, all right, I see hai
younger brother otōto

EMERGENCY SITUATIONS, EVERYDAY PHRASES, AND USEFUL ADDRESSES

EMERGENCY SITUATIONS

In an emergency, telephone **110** for the police and **119** for firefighters and ambulance service.

Japan is a relatively safe country. But here are some useful words and phrases for emergency situations.

Help!	*Tasukete!*
Fire!	*Kaji!*
Burglar!	*Dorobō!*
Pickpocket	*Suri!*
I'm lost.	*Michi ni mayotte shimaimashita.*
I'm sick.	*Byōki desu.*
Call a doctor, please.	*Isha o yonde kudasai.*
Call an ambulance, please.	*Kyūkyūsha o yonde kudasai.*
Do you understand English?	*Eigo ga wakarimasu ka?*
Do you speak English?	*Eigo o hanashimasu ka?*
Could you speak more slowly?	*Motto yukkuri hanashite kudasaimasen ka?*
Could you repeat that?	*Mō ichido, itte kudasaimasu ka?*

EVERYDAY WORDS AND PHRASES

Here are a few phrases you will use often.

Yes.	*Hai.*
No.	*Iie.*
How do you do.	*Hajimemashite.*
Pleased to meet you.	*Dōzo, yoroshiku onegai shimasu.*
Good morning.	*Ohayō gozaimasu.*
Good day.	*Konnichi wa.*
Good evening.	*Konban wa.*
Good night.	*Oyasumi nasai.*
How are you?	*Ogenki desu ka?*
I'm fine.	*Genki desu.*
Thank you.	*Arigatō gozaimasu.*
You're welcome.	*Dō itashimashite.*
No thank you.	*Kekkō desu.*
What time is it?	*Ima, nanji desu ka?*
Where am I?	*Koko wa, doko desu ka?*
What is it?	*Nan desu ka?*
Who is it?	*Dare desu ka?*
Which?	*Dore desu ka?*
Why?	*Dōshite desu ka?*
Excuse me.	*Sumimasen.*
Good bye.	*Sayōnara.*
See you again.	*De wa, mata.*
Take care.	*Ki o tsukete kudasai.*

USEFUL ADDRESSES

American citizens are not required to obtain visas for short visits to Japan. For information regarding customs, pets, and so forth, please contact the nearest office listed below.

Japanese Embassy
2520 Massachusetts Avenue, NW
Washington, D.C. 20008-2869
Tel: (202) 939-6700

Consulates General of Japan
550 West 7th Avenue, Suite 701
Anchorage, AL 99501
Tel: (907) 279-8428

350 South Grand Avenue, Suite 1700
Los Angeles, CA 90071
Tel: (213) 617-6700

50 Faremont Street, Suite 2300
San Francisco, CA 94105
Tel: (415) 777-3533

100 Colony Square Building, Suite 2000
1175 Peachtree Street, NE
Atlanta, GA 30361
Tel: (404) 892-2700

1742 Nuuana Avenue
Honolulu, HI 96817-3294
Tel: (808) 536-2226

Olympia Center, Suite 1100
737 North Michigan Avenue
Chicago, IL 60611
Tel: (312) 280-0400

Suite 2050
1 Poydras Plaza
639 Loyola Avenue
New Orleans, LA 70113
Tel: (504) 529-2101

Federal Reserve Plaza, 14th Floor
600 Atlantic Avenue
Boston, MA 02210
Tel: (617) 973-9772/3/4

2519, Commerce Tower
911 Main Street
Kansas City, MO 64105
Tel: (816) 471-0111/2/3

299 Park Avenue
New York, NY 10171
Tel: (212) 371-8222

2400 First Interstate Tower
1300 SW 5th Avenue
Portland, OR 97201
Tel: (503) 221-1811

First Interstate Bank Plaza, Suite 5300
1000 Louisiana Street
Houston, TX 77002
Tel: (713) 652-2977/8/9

Japan National Tourist Organization

The Japan National Tourist Organization provides free travel information. Its locations are as follows:

One Rockefeller Plaza, Suite 1250
New York, NY 10021
Tel: (212) 757-5640
Fax: (212) 307-6754

401 North Michigan Avenue, Suite 770
Chicago, IL 60611
Tel: (312) 222-0874
Fax: (312) 222-0876

360 Post Street, Suite 601
San Francisco, CA 94108
Tel: (415) 989-7140
Fax: (415) 398-5461

624 South Grand Avenue, Suite 1611
Los Angeles, CA 90017
Tel: (213) 623-1952
Fax: (213) 623-6301

AUSTRALIA

Japanese Embassy
112 Empire Circuit
Yarralumla, Canberra, ACT
Australia 2600
Tel: (616) 273-3244
Fax: (616) 273-1848

Japan National Tourist Organization
Level 33, The Chifley Tower
2 Chifley Square
Sydney N.S.W. 2000
Tel: (02) 232-4522
Fax: (02) 232-1494

CANADA

Japanese Embassy
225 Sussex Drive
Ottowa, Ontario K1N 9E6
Tel: (613) 241-8541
Fax: (613) 241-7415
infocul@embjapan.can.org

Consulates General of Japan
600 rue de la Gauchetiere Ouest
Suite 2120
Montreal, Quebec H3B 4L8
Tel: (514) 866-3429
Fax: (514) 395-6000

Suite 2702, Toronto–Dominion Bank Tower
P.O. Box 10, Toronto Dominion Centre
Toronto, Ontario M5K 1A1
Tel: (416) 363-5488
Fax: (416) 363-6074

10180-101 Street
Edmonton, Alberta T5J 3S4
Tel: (403) 422-3752, (403) 423-4750
Fax: (403) 424-1635

900-1177 West Hasting Street
Vancouver, B.C. V6E 2K9
Tel: (604) 684-5868
Fax: (604) 684-6939
japnvcr@istar.ca.

Japan National Tourist Organization
165 University Avenue
Toronto, Ontario M5H 3B8
Tel: (416) 366-7140
Fax: (416) 366-4530

UNITED KINGDOM

Japanese Embassy
101-104 Piccadilly, London W1V 9FN
Tel: (0171) 465-6500
Fax: (0171) 491-9347
info.@embjapan.org.uk

Consulate General of Japan
2 Melville Crescent
Edinburgh, Scotland EH3 7HW
Tel: (0131) 225-4777
Fax: (0131) 225-4828

Japan National Tourist Organization
Heathcoat House
20 Savile Row
London W1X 1AE
Tel: (0171) 734-9638
Fax: (0171) 734-4290

Bus terminals for service to Tokyo from Narita Airport.

NOTES

N O T E S

NOTES

NOTES

NOTES

N O T E S